VW Beetle Factories

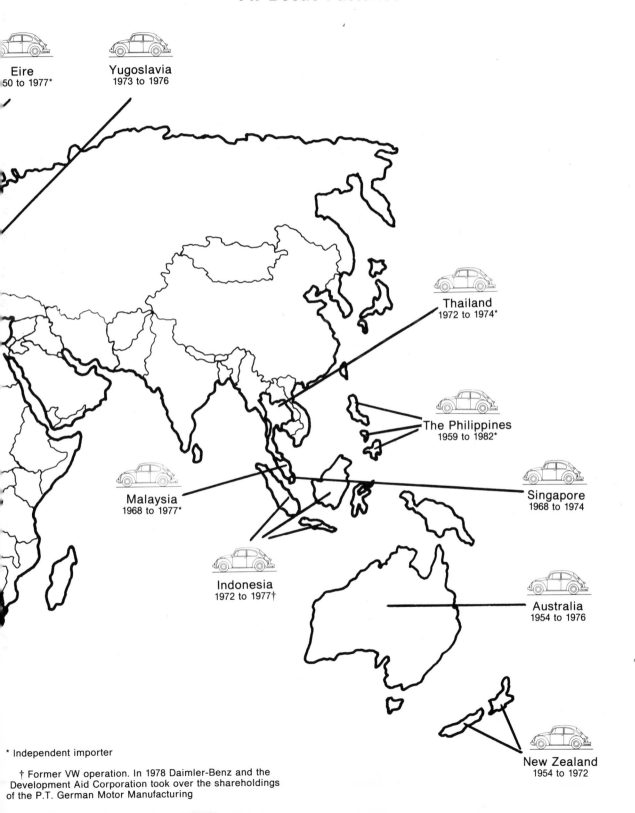

Eire
50 to 1977*

Yugoslavia
1973 to 1976

Thailand
1972 to 1974*

The Philippines
1959 to 1982*

Singapore
1968 to 1974

Malaysia
1968 to 1977*

Indonesia
1972 to 1977†

Australia
1954 to 1976

New Zealand
1954 to 1972

* Independent importer

† Former VW operation. In 1978 Daimler-Benz and the
Development Aid Corporation took over the shareholdings
of the P.T. German Motor Manufacturing

THE BEETLE

The Chronicles of the People's Car

THE BEETLE

The Chronicles of the People's Car

Volume 1:
Production and Evolution facts & figures

ETZOLD

Foulis

Haynes
®

Photographs: Etzold Archive

ISBN 0 85429 647 6

A **FOULIS** Motoring Book

First published 1985 by Verlag Bucheli as *Der Käfer I: Modelle von 1945 bis heute*
This edition published 1988

© Haynes Publishing Group 1988

Published by:
Haynes Publishing Group
Sparkford, Nr. Yeovil, Somerset
BA22 7LL, England.

Haynes Publications Inc.
861 Lawrence Drive, Newbury Park,
California 91320, USA.

British Library Cataloguing in Publication data
Etzold, H.R.
    Beetle : the definitive history.
    Vol. 1
    1. Volkswagen automobile.
    I. Title   II. Der Kafer. *English*
    629.2'222   TL215.V6
    ISBN 0-85429-647-6

Library of Congress catalog card number 87-82836

Editor: Mansur Darlington
Printed in England by: J.H. Haynes & Co.

Contents

Preface

"We are convinced that the key to success lies not in the construction of bold and wonderful new products, but in consistently and tirelessly refining even the tiniest details until maturity and perfection are reached. This is what brings truly breathtaking success." These were the words of Heinrich Nordhoff, VW's head, at a Beetle conference in Stuttgart in 1954.

By the end of the same year, 700,000 Beetles in all had been produced, and nobody even then foresaw the unparalleled production record the Beetle was to set up.

Faith was kept in the strategy of improving specific details right throughout the Beetle's production in Wolfsburg. In the period from 1948 to 1974 a total of 78,000 modifications were carried out on the Beetle. Even the tiniest details were tended to with love, and, from time to time, the necessary high cost.

According to my own researches, there has been only one detail on the Beetle that has never been altered. It is the cross-section of the metal channel that holds the rubber strip to seal the bonnet and boot.

The task of this book is to list the most important modifications with their corresponding date of inception and chassis number, so that those who want precise information or would like to restore a Beetle, will have a comprehensive reference book at hand.

H.-R. Etzold

Publisher's note
The Publisher would like to thank Robin Wager (Editor of the magazine *VW Motoring)* for his contribution as technical editor of this book, and in bringing to bear his expertise to the translating into English intractable German technical terminology.

Beetle Models from 1945

It is a tradition at the Volkswagen factory that an updated model in unveiled after the long company holidays. Nevertheless, the date of unveiling has, from time to time, been set for October or January; and, moreover, many specific improvements are, of course, incorporated into the series during the production year. For this reason the modifications in the following lists are summarized for a particular production year. Noted down is the chassis number, and the date when the modification was introduced.

In the German edition of this book, engine output was expressed using the metric DIN unit PS. This has been translated throughout the main text as bhp which is more familiar to English readers. For technical accuracy, however, PS has been retained in the appendices. For an exact conversion from PS to bhp, multiply the PS figure by 0.986.

1945–1948

In the years between 1945 and 1948 there is no visible change in the bodywork. Those who have the necessary coupons can buy the 1946 Beetle for 5,000 Reichsmarks (or after the Currency Reform for 5,300 Deutschemarks). The paintwork, in grey, blue and black, is matt, since better quality paint cannot be had at this time.

On 14 October 1946 the 10,000th Beetle produced since the end of the war rolls off the production line. The workers celebrate the event with the slogan: *10,000 Wagen – nichts im Magen – wer kann das ertragen?* literally: 10,000 cars – empty bellies – who can bear it?

Dates and facts

1945	10.4.	The Americans march in – at this time 17,109 people are living in the town – many in emergency accommodation. The factory employs 9,000 workers. By the end of the war around 336,000 Volkswagen-savers* have contributed a total of 267 million Marks. The German Labour Front placed these savings contributions in a special account at the Workers' Bank.
	25.5.	At its first sitting the council of representatives of the town appointed by the British military government decides to give the VW-town the name 'Wolfsburg'.
		The Volkswagen factory is temporarily renamed the Wolfsburg Motor Works. According to statute No. 52 of the military government the company's assets are seized.
	May/ June	Work begins again on a limited scale. Besides repair work on English army vehicles, by the end of the year 1,785 Volkswagens are produced, destined

Dates and facts

		exclusively for use by the occupying powers, and (as temporary delivery vans) by the German Postal Service.
1946		10,020 Volkswagens are produced during the whole year.
1947		Out of the year's total production (8,987) 56 Saloons are exported to the Netherlands. From 8 August onwards the brothers Pon become VW General Importers for the Netherlands.
1948	1.1.	Heinrich Nordhoff (Dipl. Eng.) takes over the running of the factory as General Manager.
	May	The 25,000th Volkswagen rolls off the production line.
	29.7.	The Company moves its registered headquarters, originally in Berlin, to Wolfsburg.
	7.10.	The Association of Former Volkswagen Savers (*Hilfsverein ehemaliger Volkswagensparer e.V. Niedermarsburg*) is founded, and there is a complaint from two VW savers that they have not received their cars.

*On 1 August 1938 a savings scheme was introduced intended to help aspiring VW owners to save the purchase price.

The 1948 Beetle

Rear axle with single-acting shock absorbers until 1951

Boot lid with external T-handle until 1949

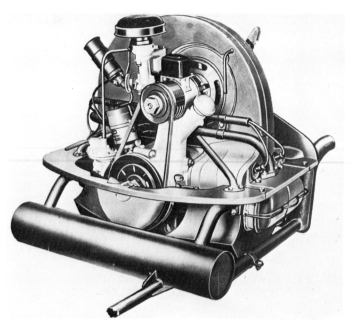

1.1-litre engine. Cooling air throttle valve with
swing-handle until 1950

Pull-out door-handle until 1959

Licence-plate
pressing on
rear lid until
1949

10

1945–1948 The most important modifications

Year	Chassis No.	Assembly No.	Modification
Engine/clutch/heating			
1943	–	020000	Engine increased from 985 cc to 1131 cc. Sealing tubes for push rods: corrugated tube-ends, previously sprung.
1946	054 617	–	
1947	071 616	099610	Cooling air throttle valve: previously slide valve, now choke valve with swing handle.
1948 April 48	076 722	105558	Crankshaft: with 48.5 mm/dia for flywheel. Flywheel with 48.5 mm bore.
Fuel system			
1946	057 390	–	Fuel tank: fitted higher
Front axle/Steering			
1946	057 011	–	Lubrication nipples on inner trackrod joints: facing left rear wheel, and no longer at right angles to track rod.
Brakes/Wheels/Tyres			
1946	059 107	–	Brake cable: with lubrication nipple, previously without. Tyres: 5.00 x 16; before 4.50 x 16.
Chassis			
1940 3.8.1940	000 026	–	Chassis number: inscribed by hand on the flat surface at the front of the Chassis.
1945 16.5.45	052 016	–	Chassis number: inscribed by hand on the right-hand side on the chassis tunnel below rear seat
1948	073 816	–	Choke cable: unsprung.
Bodywork			
1946	057 893	066991	Suppression of engine noise: cardboard for noise reduction in engine compartment.
1947	071 377	10707	Fastenings for spare-wheel: bracket for chain & lock.

Year	Chassis No.	Assembly No.	Modification
General Modifications			
1942	–	–	Schwimmwagen: 511 vehicles manufactured
1943	–	–	Schwimmwagen: 8258 vehicles manufactured
1944	–	–	Schwimmwagen: 458 vehicles manufactured per month
1947 13.10.47	073 348	–	Chassis No.: imprinted with a stencil on chassis tunnel between gear lever and hand-brake.
1948	075 840	–	Chassis No.: between hand-brake and gear lever, imprinted with a stencil on chassis tunnel

1949

Crucial to the Beetle's future success is the decision to export the Volkswagen. The first country with whom export contracts are signed is Holland in 1947.

To cater for the tastes of the foreign automobile customer, the new export model is introduced to the market in July 1949. It can be distinguished from the Standard model by its chrome-finished bumpers, hub caps, headlamp rims and door handles. The bumpers are curved, and, the sickle-shaped bumper overriders are exchanged for a more rounded and compact design. The instrument panel stays practically the same; the export saloon, however, is fitted with a two-spoke steering wheel. The right inset of the dashboard, previously pressed in one piece with the rest of the dashboard, now has a moulded blanking piece. Now, if you should want to install a radio or a clock, you no longer need to saw out the sheet metal.

Interior fittings and upholstery of the Export saloon are of a better quality. For the first time the Beetle is available with high-gloss paintwork. The front bonnet latch (formerly opened with a straight handle) is now opened from the car interior. From June of this year the front seats can be adjusted when driving. From October onwards the Beetle comes without the previously standard starting-crank, and also the number plate pressing in the engine lid.

On 13 May 1949 the 50,000th Volkswagen rolls off the assembly line. The Export model brought out on 1 July 1949 costs 5450 DM. In the same year Karmann present the four-seater Beetle Cabriolet.

Dates and facts

1949	8.1.	This is when we see the first VW Beetle shipped to Holland. Destination: the United States of America. Now begins the Beetle's victory march into the USA.
	13.5.	The 50,000th Volkswagen built since the end of the war rolls off the line.
	30.6.	To increase turnover the new subsidiary, the Volkswagen Finance Company (Volkswagen Finanzierungsgesellschaft) is formed.
	1.7.	The Export model, a VW Beetle with improved fitting, is produced: it costs 5450 DM. At the same time Karmann shows its newly assembled four-seater Cabriolet.
	6.9.	In directive No.202, the military government relinquishes control of the assets it had formerly seized, which included those of the Volkswagen concern.

In July the Export model is introduced. It is distinguishable from the outside by its additional chromework: chrome trim on running-boards, waist-line and bonnet. In the front mudguards are two round decorative grilles, and the horn is fitted under the mudguard.

Export dashboard. Glove compartment and instrument panels with chrome trim. Two-spoke steering wheel. Control knobs of ivory-coloured plastic. The bonnet is opened by means of a pull knob inside the vehicle.

On the engine lid the pressing for the number plate is dropped. The lid can no longer be locked.

Standard dashboard. On the right-hand side of instrument panel is a blanking plate. The sheet metal need no longer be sawn out if a radio is to be fitted. Under the left instrument panel the pull knob to open the bonnet is located.

Luggage compartment with two longitudinal metal rails, formerly without metal rails.

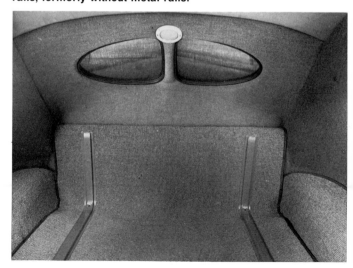

14

Air filter: former pan-shaped filter replaced by one of mushroom-shaped design.

Until October 1949 small throttle pedal roller.

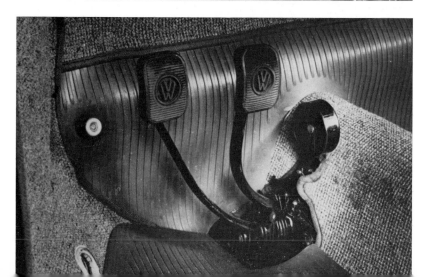

From October 1949 large throttle pedal roller.

15

On 3.6.1949 production
begins *en masse* of four-
seater Beetle Cabrio by
Karmann. One to two
models are manufactured
daily.

In 1949 the production
begins of the Hebmüller
Cabrio. Since the vehicle
is fitted with a fully retractable roof, there is only
'occasional' rear seating
provided.

Cutaway illustration of the
Export Beetle.

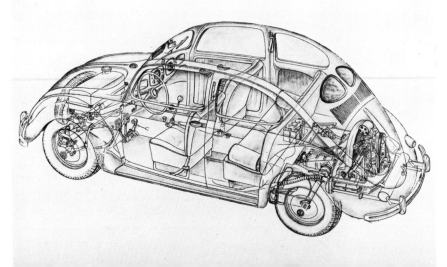

1949
The most important modifications

Year	Chassis No.	Assembly No.	Modification
Engine/clutch/heating			
5.1.49	091914	–	Heating conduit: double heating conduit.
14.1.49	092918	123564	Air filter: pan-shaped filter replaced by new mushroom-shaped design.
18.1.49	093270	124031	Warm air conduit – lower part: modified heat flap without hinge.
1.2.49	094554	125426	Intake pipe bracket.
7.3.49	096978	128051	Air cooling fan: control discontinued.
8.4.49	100826	132017	Fuel pump: with blue Solex diaphragms fitted with 4 gaskets.
28.4.49	101902	133131	Exhaust valves with case-hardened stems on all models, except engine number 133 634-668.
June 1949	1-0 106637	137701	Breather pipe.
June 1949	1-0 108091	139293	Filter: in ventilation holes of cylinder head.
July 1949	1-0 114186	–	Felt cone air filter for engines in Volkswagen Type 11A.
Sept. 1949	1-0 119588	150702	Piston clearance for No. 3 cylinder 0.05 mm greater.
Sept. 1949	1-0 120959	152050	Clutch disc: radially ribbed clutch disc (F + S). Initially still double pressure springs.
Oct 1949	–	–	Starting handle discontinued.
Dec. 1949	1-0 136729	168075	Pushrod tubes: corrugations now only at ends, which are both cylindrical.
Fuel system			
18.1.49	092879	–	Petrol stop cock; formerly with cork seal, now with Thiokol seal.
Aug. 1949	1-0 116375	116021	Fuel tank shape changed, central tap, filter discontinued.
Aug. 1949	–	–	Fuel filler cap: with VW emblem, sealing strengthened, locking spring reinforced.
Front axle/steering			
15.3.49	097580	from 106047 to 107046	Torsion bars: lower 5-leaf, upper 4-leaf (1000 experimental front axles); instead of as before: lower 4-leaf, upper 5-leaf.
14.4.49	101322	110007	Torsion bars: lower 5-leaf, upper 4-leaf, on all models; formerly: lower 4-leaf, upper 5-leaf.

Year	Chassis No.	No.	Modification
Aug. 1949	1-0 117053	125338	Front axle: front and rear reinforced double-acting telescopic shock absorbers. Support tubes and torsion bars (4/5) shortened, side plates longer.
Sept. 1949	1-0 123476	131907	Track rod, right: with left- and right-hand thread, as standard.

Rear axle/gears

Year	Chassis No.	No.	Modification
March 1949	from 098396 to 098400	from 108551 to 109028	Gear box: Electron, on some models formerly, refined magnesium-aluminium alloy
17.3.49	098400	108553	Gearbox oil topping up: 2.5 litres, instead of 3 litres as before.
26.4.49	102026	112521	Gearbox: Electron, standard: formerly refined magnesium-aluminium alloy.
Aug. 1949	1-0 117053	–	Lever type shock absorbers double-acting, on some models. Formerly single-acting.
Oct. 1949	1-0 127560	137582	Clutch lever: reinforced construction.

Bodywork

Year	Chassis No.	No.	Modification
25.1.49	093781	–	Front seat: backrest straight; former position, slanted.
9.2.49	094470	44221	Luggage space: two metal rails lengthwise instead of being without rails.
1.5.49	1-0 102948	56912	Dashboard inset for radio: Bakelite blanking plate. Bonnet lid: with a latch (Bowden cable); formerly locking handle. Engine lid no longer lockable. Formerly locking handle. Rear and front bumpers: wider section; the manufacture of the convex curved bumper overriders is stopped.
6.5.49	1-0 102383	52070	Dashboard: completely changed, 2-spoke steering wheel, clock (Export model).
9.5.49	1-0 103168	53453	Glove compartment: Fibre material secured with a strap. Formerly sheet metal.
June 1949	–	–	Rear window: glass specification changed.

Year	Chassis No.	No.	Modification
June 1949	–	–	Rear view mirror: secured to avoid vibration.
2.6.49	1-0 106636	–	Paintwork: synthetic, formerly cellulose.
July 1949	1-0 111054	60759	Engine lid inset for number plate dropped.
Aug. 1949	1-0 117700	67337	Armrest on left-hand door discontinued.
Oct. 1949	1-0 124032	73554	Floor covering: brown-coloured front moulded rubber mats, and rubber footwell panelling. Rear rubber mats discontinued.

Chassis

Year	Chassis No.	No.	Modification
5.1.49	091914	–	Heater cable: from single to double heater cable.
25.1.49	093834	–	Throttle cable: elbow at front end: formerly, eye.
29.4.49	102537	–	Pedal bearing: additional lubrication nipple on alloy bearings.
6.5.49	1-0 103039	R.109131	Heater cables: conduit ends with rubber stoppers.
22.6.49	1-0 107101	R.115523	Chassis number: printed on the smooth surface of the frame tunnel lengthwise with die.
Oct. 1949	1-0 128058	–	Accelerator pedal: larger roller.
Oct. 1949	1-0 128116	R.135264	Runner for driver's seat left: raised 15 mm.

Electrics

Year	Chassis No.	No.	Modification
6.5.49	1-0 102848	K.56612	Fuse box: formerly under the instrument panel, now on the left front side panel.
May 1949	1-0 106717	K.56078	Bulb for brake light: 6 volts, 15 watt.
June 1949	1-0 106717	K.56343	Reflectors: more protection in the wet.
28.8.49	1-0 102651	–	Chassis No. seven digit number. Formerly six digits.
2.6.49	1-0 106636	–	VW Export Saloon production begins.
3.6.49	1-0 099906	–	VW Cabriolet production begins.
Aug. 1949	1-0 116616	–	Running-in sticker: dropped from windscreen.
Oct. 1949	–	–	Tool kit: starting handle discontinued.

1950

This year the door window glasses are given a curved cut-out to aid draught-free ventilation. The sunroof is also new this year. "The term 'sliding roof' as applied to the model to be found in the VW is not quite accurate. To be precise, it is a folding roof," as VW specialist Arthur Westrup put it in 1950 in his book *Drive better with the Volkswagen*. The extra cost for the sunroof amounts to 250 DM.

In the same year hydraulic brakes are introduced in the Export model.

The Volkswagen workforce celebrates the production of the 100,000th Beetle in 1950. The customer can choose between the Standard model for 5050 DM and the Export model for 5700 DM. The statistics for vehicle registration in the Federal Republic show VW on its own at the top with 41.5 per cent. On average 342 Volkswagens are produced daily. The Auto Union achieves a market share of 1.1 per cent in the Federal Republic, Opel 21.6 per cent.

The VW workforce, averaged over the year, has grown to 13,305 employees. Statistically, there are 6.82 cars produced per man. The average hourly wage in West Germany (coal mining excluded) comes to 1.24 DM, the workers at VW receive 1.50 DM.

Dates and Facts

1950	Feb.	The first Volkswagen Transporter, a completely new type of vehicle, rolls off the production line: full scale production begins on 8 March with 10 vehicles per day.
	4.3.	100,000th Volkswagen since the end of the war.

From 28.4.1950 the Beetle is available on request with a folding sunroof.

For better ventilation the door windows have a curved cut-out.

From 3.6.1950 an ashtray is located above the starter button in the Export model.

In contrast to the Export Saloon, in which, from 1949, the horn is located under the left mudguard, on the Standard Saloon it remains attached to the bumper bracket outside. For this reason the mudguards on the Standard Saloon have no decorative grilles.

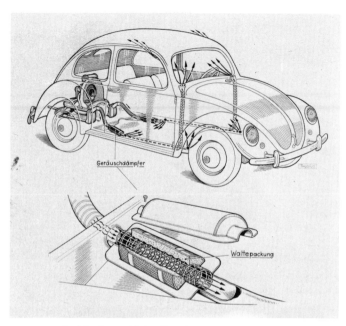

Geräuschdämpfer

Wattepackung

Inside the vehicle: Heating pipe with noise suppressors.

Automatic cooling air regulation. The air control valve is controlled via a thermostat according to the engine temperature.

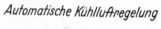

Automatische Kühlluftregelung

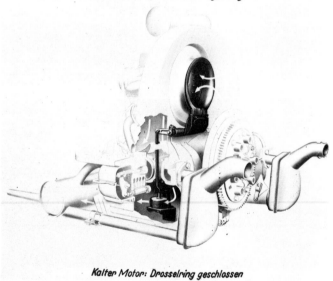

Kalter Motor: Drosselring geschlossen

Front axle: spring assembly 5-leaf above and below.

In the early years of the Beetle the shape of the air filter was constantly changing. From October 1950 a filter with felt insert was used.

1950

The most important modifications

Year	Chassis No.	No.	Modification
Engine/clutch/heating			
Jan. 50	1-0138765	170086	Crankcase: oil can be drained completely (breached control chamber). Oil level 2.51: oil splash guard dropped; No. 4 main bearing has a groove.
Jan. 50	1-0140243	–	Cylinders: gasket between cylinder and cylinder head.
17.1.50	1-0141601	173030	Dip-stick: phosphated and blackened.
Feb. 50	–	–	Oil drain plug with 19 mm hexagonal head, on some models.
30.3.50	1-0156129	188974	Exhaust tailpipe diameter increased from 31 mm to 32 mm.
2.5.50	1-0162580	196110	Automatic cooling-air regulation: formerly control valve with swivel handle.
9.5.50	1-0164402	198222	Exhaust box: connecting pipe on exhaust box (for greater preheating of fuel-air mixture) standard.
13.5.50	–	199321	Piston: installation of Mahle Autothermic piston (on some models).
19.6.50	1-0173719	108481	Clutch: now with only single springs, standard.
10.8.50	1-0183539	220317	Exhaust valve: hardened standard.
Oct. 50	–	–	Oil filter: mechanical oil filter (service part).
16.11.50	1-0210317	from 252752 to 253775	Exhaust valves: with welded heads.
Front axle/steering			
Jan. 50	1-0138835	147306	Torsion bars: upper and lower 5-leaf instead of as before upper 4-leaf, lower 5-leaf.
Aug. 50	1-0183052	125336	Shock absorbers with fluid reservoir (Hemscheidt) for old design front axle (service part).
Rear axle/gears			
28.5.50	1-0167890	180741	Brake cylinders: 15.8 mm diameter
Brakes/wheels/tyres			
March 50	1-0155322	–	Hydraulic brakes; on some models (Type 11A ± 15)
April 50	1-0158253	–	Hydraulic brakes standard (Type 11A + 15).

Year	Chassis No.	Assembly No.	Modification
13.5.50	1-0164460	–	Brake fluid reservoir with float; formerly: with filter.
20.5.50	1-0167890	–	Hydraulic brakes: diameter of brake master cylinder reduced from 22.2 mm to 19.5 mm. Diameter of rear wheel brake cylinder reduced from 19.05 mm to 15.9 mm.

Chassis

Year	Chassis No.	Assembly No.	Modification
10.2.50	1-0146222	–	Accelerator cable: pin and clip at front. Formerly: elbow.
24.3.50	1-0154928	R162801	Chassis number: Die-stamped on rear left on vertical sidepanel of crossmember. Formerly: die-stamped longitudinally on smooth surface of chassis tunnel.
29.4.50	1-0162444	–	Handle for heater flap cable: turn-handle.
May 50	–	–	Heating ducts with noise suppression.
12.9.50	1-0192742	–	Accelerator cable: for compression spring, standard.
17.10.50	1-0202071	–	Handbrake lever shorter.

Bodywork

Year	Chassis No.	Assembly No.	Modification
Jan. 50	1-0140130	89257	Boot lock cable: larger knob.
26.1.50	1-0143276	92290	Front wing: sealing ring between headlight and wing.
13.2.50	1-0146657	95531	Floor covering, rear: brown-coloured moulded rubber mats. Formerly: cord carpets.
3.4.50	1-0156991	105431	Ventilation, draught-free: changes to upper window channel, the horizontal window channel, the window raiser, and the top of window glass.
18.4.50	1-0159782	108281	Doorlock, right: locking handle.
3.6.50	1-0169714	118146	Ashtray: on dashboard and sidepanel, rear right.

Electrics

Year	Chassis No.	Assembly No.	Modification
Jan. 50	1-0140537	K.89656	Warning lights on dashboard: for indicator and main beam, left; generator and oil warning, right.

General modifications

Year	Chassis No.	Assembly No.	Modification
28.4.50	–	–	VW Saloon with sunroof: production begins.

1951

The 1951 Beetle is easily recognisable by the side ventilation flaps in the A-panels. The standard model is available in mid-blue and pearl grey. 75 per cent of customers decide on grey.

The Export model is distinguished not only by additional decorative trim around the windscreen, but also by the Wolfsburg crest emblazoned on the bonnet.

In the Export model and the Cabrio the lever shock absorbers are replaced by telescopic shock absorbers, and the standard model is run in on the test bench rather than on the road.

The bolster cushions for the rear seats fall victim to the new refurbishment brief: "they gave the passengers the feeling of being in a boudoir". Also the toolkit comes without the wheel nuts. In October the 250,000th Volkswagen rolls off the line; 93,709 Beetles are produced this year. The cheapest Beetle costs 4600 DM.

Revenue from Export trade reaches 121.6 Million DM. 35,742 Volkswagens are exported to 29 countries. Main buyers are Belgium, Sweden, Switzerland, Holland, Finland and Brazil. In the Federal Republic there are 729 VW garages, employing a total of 11,121 mechanics.

Dates and facts

1951	5.10.	The 250,000th Volkswagen since the end of the war is built.

Ventilation flaps in the side panels

Export model with additional trim around the windscreen.

Export model: Wolfsburg crest on the bonnet.

On the rear axle for the export model, double-acting telescopic shock absorbers instead of lever type single-acting shock absorbers.

On 20.11.1951 rear seat bolster cushions (in mass production on the Export model since 1949) are discontinued.

Battery secured by two springs, which clip onto hooks in the lid.

1951   The most important modifications

Year	Chassis No.	Assembly No.	Modification
Engine/clutch/heating			
18.1.51	1-0224763	–	Acclerator cable: sleeve for guiding return spring.
19.1.51	1-0225376	272061	Crankcase: magnesium-aluminium alloy replaced by Elektron.
21.3.51	1-0241734	287661	Camshaft gear built from synthetic material (Resitax). (Export models only).
27.3.51	1-0242600	293200	Exhaust silencer: pipe modified.
6.4.51	1-0243731	294845	Heater flaps: front heater flaps moved inside the heat exchangers.
18.4.51	1-0246090	297815	Generator uprated from AL15 to RED 130/6-2600 AL16.
April 51	–	296606	Crankcase: windows are installed in both halves of crankcase.
26.11.51	1-0305813	369483	Valve seat for exhaust valve of V2 A-steel, standard.
27.11.51	1-0306417	from 370472 to 370556	Valves: with caps, on some models.
Rear axle/gears			
6.4.51	1-0244003	274520	Shock absorbers: telescopic shock absorbers. Formerly lever shock absorbers (only on Export models and Cabrio).
Chassis			
31.7.51	1-0272406	–	Hand brake lever covered by rubber boot on chassis tunnel.
Bodywork			
6.1.51	1-0221638	168482	Ventilation flaps fitted on front side panels.
1.4.51	1-0243731	–	Bonnet: Wolfsburg crest.
12.4.51	1-0244668	190177	Windscreen: with trim.
13.4.51	1-0241638	–	Car ventilation: front left- and right-hand side panels have pull-out flaps. Bonnet: Bowden cable release: formerly handle. Glove compartment (151) lockable. Doors (151): concealed door hinges. Door trim (151): one side pocket on each.

Year	Chassis No.	Assembly No.	Modification
14.8.51	1-0276126	–	Ventilation flaps: New mesh screen and operating lever.
25.10.51	1-0296592	309965	Strengthened jacking points.
20.11.51	1-0304210	–	Rear seat bolster cushions discontinued.

Electrics

Year	Chassis No.	Assembly No.	Modification
4.1.51	1-0221051	266644	Generator pulley modified to prevent v-belt jumping off.
March 51	–	–	Distributor marked with number/letter according to month/year.
13.4.51	1-0241638	–	Interior light (151) given additional door switch. Cut-out switch accessible when cover removed.
18.4.51	1-0246090	297815	Generator now RED 130/6 2600 AL16. Formerly AL15.
1.12.51	1-0308653	–	Dashboard indicator lamp now 6 volt, 0.6 watt. Formerly 6 volt, 1.2 watt.

General modifications

Year	Chassis No.	Assembly No.	Modification
5.2.51	1-0229182	–	Standard saloon run in only on the test bench.
24.9.51	1-0287416	–	Toolkit: wheel bolts discontinued.

1952

This year's model has quarter-lights in the front doors. The bumpers are of deeper section and fitted with two impact-resistant overriders.

The opening for the concealed horn under the left-hand mudguard is covered with an oval grille painted to match the rest of the car.

On the bonnet the old vertical handle is replaced by a T-shaped handle.

The rear lights have two top-mounted lenses for the brake lights. The brake and rear light fuse is moved from the engine compartment to the rear of the dashboard.

The Export model is trimmed with polished aluminium strips on the boot and wider smooth strips (without ribs) along the body-line. In addition there is bright trim on door, side and rear windows and oval grilles in bright aluminium for the horn openings in the front mudguards. The boot handle is redesigned, and the dashboard has undergone a transformation. The left-hand glove compartment is discontinued but an extra door pocket is added. The indicator switch is now to the left of the steering wheel. The starter button is also to the left, while the choke is now located on the dashboard to the right of the wheel.

The lights and wipers are operated by pull switches. Switches under the instrument panel operate the instrument and interior lights. To achieve better illumination the interior light is moved from the rear to the left roof cant rail.

On Export models a black horn button with the Wolfsburg crest in gold is fitted to a chrome ring in the steering wheel.

From this date the saloon runs on small but fatter tyres (5.00 – 16 replaced by 5.60 – 15). To reduce noise, the bulkhead separating the luggage space from the engine compartment is fitted with a board sprayed with sound-proofing material.

The ride is improved by the six-leaf torsion bars in the front suspension, as well as modified front and rear suspension. On the Export models there is also synchromesh on 2nd, 3rd and 4th gears.

For better preheating of the fuel-air mixture, the exhaust heater tube directly contacts the inlet manifold and is connected by an aluminium casting.

41.4 per cent of all Beetles are exported. The hourly wage at the VW factory has meanwhile risen to 2.13 DM. In the fourth quarter the daily production reaches 734. The most expensive Beetle costs 4,600 DM.

Dates and facts

1952	11.9.	Founding of the Volkswagen Canada sales organization.

Bumper with deep section and impact-resistant
bumper overriders. Oval grilles for concealed
horns.

Right: ventilation provided by quarter lights.

Completely new dashboard; left-hand glovebox
discontinued.

Glovebox with lid. Passenger side ashtray.

Starter button and indicator switch to left of steering wheel.

Speedometer of 110 mm diameter. Warning lights built into dial.

Export model: deep black horn button with golden Wolfsburg crest. Chrome plated surround in centre of wheel.

Engine cover with horizontal T-handle.

Rear lights with heart-shaped lenses for brake lights. The reversing light illustrated is not standard equipment.

Rear view of 1953 Model.

Below right: Turn-handle for heating system.

32

Choke button on chassis tunnel discontinued.

Engine with 28 PCI carburettor fitted with accelerator pump for first time.

Door trim with stitched lines on upper section and bright trim.

Front luggage compartment with view of new dashboard from reverse side.

1952 The most important modifications

Year	Chassis No.	Assembly No.	Modification
Engine/clutch/heating			
21.1.52	1-0320 804	387 815	Hollow bolt with felt ring to prevent grease leakage.
25.3.52	1-0338 059	408 661	Connecting pipe between tailpipe and exhaust silencer discontinued
29.5.52	1-0357 667	433 033	Valve springs: the previous two springs are now replaced by one.
20.8.52	1-0382 029	–	Oil bath air filter fitted on some models.
1.10.52	1-0397 023	481 713	Heating adjustment by rotary knob and spindle. Inlet manifold combined with exhaust heating pipe in aluminium casting.
15.10.52	1-0402 III	–	
20.10.52	–	122-00 001	VW industrial engine: production begins.
Fuel system			
1.10.52	1-0397 023	481 713	Carburettor 28 PCI. Formerly 26 VFIS.
Nov. 52	–		Felt cone air filter now with flame-trap.
Front axle/steering			
1.10.52	1-0397 023	4.10.951	Suspension and front axle: torsion-bars 6-leaf instead of previously: 2x5-leaf. Shock absorber travel increased to 130 mm, from 90 mm.
Rear axle/transmission			
1.10.52	1-0397 023	A-0000I	Synchromesh gears now 2nd, 3rd and 4th for VW Export Saloon; formerly standard gears. Gearbox mounting: rubber/steel mountings front and rear. Formerly without rubber/steel mountings. Torsion bar diameter reduced from 25 to 24 mm.
Brakes/wheels/tyres			
7.2.52	1-0324 758	–	Hydraulic brake reservoir now without float.

Year	Chassis No.	Assembly No.	Modification
1.10.52	1-0397023	VA410951 HA000001 HA456614	Tyres: 5.60 – 15; wheel rims 4J – 15, formerly 5.00 – 16. Tyre pressure: 1.1 bar at front; at rear 1.4 or 1.6 bar. Rear wheel brake cylinder diameter increased from 15.9 mm to 17.5 mm.

Chassis

Year	Chassis No.	Assembly No.	Modification
22.1.52	1-0316900	–	Handbrake lever: boot on chassis tunnel (Export only).
20.6.52	1-0365201	HA418210	Clutch cable adjusting nut: diameter reduced; clutch operating lever with conical eye.
1.10.52	1-0397023	R415437 HA000001 HA456614	Heating: rotary knob with fine adjustment.

Bodywork

Year	Chassis No.	Assembly No.	Modification
1.10.52	1-0397023	337823	Quarter light in both doors. Heating: broader demister nozzles for windscreen. Heating outlet: with rotary knob and spindle. Formerly pull knob. Silencing: padding in front of engine bay. Crank-operated window: $3^{1}/_{4}$ turns. Formerly $10^{1}/_{2}$. Engine lid: T-handle. Formerly vertical handle. Bumpers: broad profile, heavy-duty overriders. Mouldings anodized and polished. Formerly aluminium mouldings. Glove compartment with lid and push button. Formerly open compartment. Dashboard completely redesigned. Rubber floor mats, with press studs, non-slip. Fittings: ashtray at front for passenger; different cloth patterns.

Electrics

Year	Chassis No.	Assembly No.	Modification
20.2.52	1-0322639	–	Parking light in headlight: new: parking light, terminal 58 of standard wiring system. Formerly terminal 57.
1.10.52	1-0397023	481713	Brake lights: lenses on top of light cluster: combined with tail lights and reflectors. Formerly single light in centre of engine cover. Fuse box for brake/tail lights on reverse side of dashboard.

Windscreen wiper: wider sweep, with more power; self-parking (Export only). Battery 70 Ah; clamping strap longitudinal. Formerly 84 Ah; clamping strap at right angles to direction of travel. Starter button to left of steering wheel on dashboard. Formerly right of steering wheel.
Indicator switch lever on left of steering column. Formerly switch on dashboard. Lights and wiper switch: one pull-switch for each. Formerly rotary switch. Internal and instrument lighting: toggle switch underneath instrument panel. Horn: new concealed installation for Standard and Export with decorative grille. Formerly exterior fitting. Speedometer: larger dial with warning lights. Internal light above left door pillar. Formerly above driving mirror. Plug socket for inspection lamp discontinued. Formerly installed under the dashboard. Horn button/steering wheel now with Wolfsburg crest.

General Modifications

Year	Chassis No.	Assembly No.	Modification
19.3.52	1-0336561	–	Took-kit: *'Klettermaxe' jack*.
1.10.52	1-0397023	–	Tool-kit: spare V-belt dropped.
15.10.52	1-0402111	–	Tool-kit: spare V-belt included.

1953

A significant date in the history of the Beetle is 10 March 1953. On this day the central rib is removed from the rear window from chassis no. 1-0454951 onwards. The new standard window is 23 per cent larger and oval in shape. The spare parts industry follows suit and develops a one-piece window for retro-fitting. If you have anything about you, and are the owner of an old model Beetle, you go ahead and saw out the central rib and install the more modern window.

The interior light has a switch, so that the light can be turned off even when the door is open.

The pull-out ashtray has an additional handle and is thereby easier to open. Even the Standard model is now mass-produced with this type of ashtray.

The tiny opening of the petrol filler neck is increased again from 40 to 80 mm. An an optional extra a steering damper can be installed.

When the 500,000th car rolls off the line in July 1953, the workforce receives a bonus of 2.5 million marks.

The Volkswagen company's share of private vehicle production in the Federal republic amounts to 42.5 per cent. 68,754 vehicles are exported; revenue from foreign exchange brings in 254.2 million marks.

The average daily production including Transporter manufacture stands at 673 vehicles.

In Brazil, Volkswagen do Brasil S.A. is formed in São Paulo, and develops into one of the most important subsidiaries. On 8 December 1953, the 250,000th visitor since the end of the war comes to view the Wolfsburg factory. The VW workforce has grown to 20,569 employees.

Dates and facts

1953	23.3.	Volkswagen do Brazil S.A. formed São Bernardo do Campo near São Paulo for the manufacture of Volkswagens in Brazil.
	20.4.	Founding of the charitable/ public utility 'VW home building project'.
	3.7.	The 500,000th Volkswagen rolls off the line.

Rear window without central rib.

The rear window is oval in shape, and 23 per cent larger than the previous *Brezelfenster* (pretzel-window).

Cutaway of the 1953 Beetle.

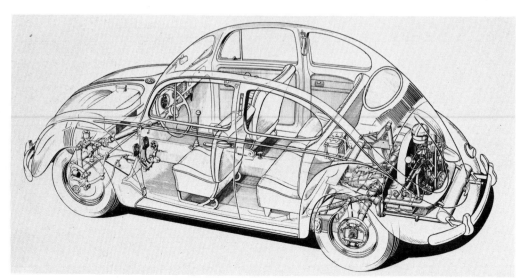

All Beetle models are fitted with an oil-bath air filter.

Above left:
Ashtray in dashboard, with small handle.

The neck of the petrol tank is enlarged from 40 to 80 mm.

Beetle Cabrio, 1954.

1953   The most important modifications

Year	Chassis No.	Assembly No.	Modification
Engine/clutch/heating			
2.1.53	1-0428221	–	Oil-bath air filter: with clamping strap.
15.1.53	1-0433397	525661	Carburettor: air correction jet 200. Formerly 190.
20.1.53	1-0435509	528095	Valve clearance reduced from 0.15 mm to 0.10 mm.
21.12.53	1-0575415	695282	Engine performance and capacity increased from 25 HP/1131 cm³ to 30 HP/1192 cm³. Compression ratio from 5.8:1 to 6.1:1. Oil-bath air filter installed on all models. Engine running-in requirement discontinued.
Fuel system			
15.1.53	1-0433397	518653	Carburettor 28 PCI: ball check-valves bronze. Formerly steel.
7.3.53	1-0454951	392967	Fuel tank filler neck 80 mm. Formerly 40 mm.
Front axle/steering			
21.8.53	1-0517304	531623	Front axle torsion bars 8-leaf. Formerly 6-leaf.
21.8.53	1-0517880	532264	Front wheel bearing caps no longer filled with grease.
21.11.53	1-0562054	–	Steering wheel construction: two spokes pointing downwards, view of speedo unrestricted.
Brakes/wheels/tyres			
21.12.53	1-0575415 (Exp) 1-0575417 (Stand.)	VA590166 HA167878	Brake fluid reservoir for brake master cylinder in front luggage bay behind spare wheel. Formerly on brake master cylinder.
Bodywork			
14.2.53	1-0441708	380257	Door striker plate adjustable. Formerly: non-adjustable.
10.3.53	1-0454951	392967	Trim moulding of Reflectal. Rear window 23 per cent larger and curved. Formerly window with central rib. Safety glass. Formerly plate glass. Ashtray with handle on dashboard (Standard also).
20.3.53	1-0448117	12410	VW Cabriolet: adjustable door striker plate.
18.6.53	1-0495968	431450	Windscreen wiper construction: hole for wiper shaft set 8 mm deeper.

Year	Chassis No.	Assembly No.	Modification
			Boot lid support shorter, changing angle of open lid. Bearing sealing for windscreen wiper shaft incorporating sealing compound.
6.7.53	1-0503371 1-0503276	438200 (Exp) 438295 (Std)	Quarter-light catches with locks.
July 53	1-0509668	–	Rear view mirror integral with sun visor.
21.12.53	1-0575415 1-0575417 (Stand.)		Heating outlets now at front, and larger with protective grille. Formerly two outlets in rear.

Frame

Year	Chassis No.	Assembly No.	Modification
3.11.53	1-0552991 (Stand.)		Heater control knob without inscription.

Electrics

Year	Chassis No.	Assembly No.	Modification
3.2.53	1-0441556	K380297	Fuses: fuse wire made from brass.
10.3.53	1-0454951	K392967	Interior light with off-switch; 10 watt bulb. Formerly 5 watt. Speedometer indicator arrow new: combined and broader. Formerly: separate.
9.10.53	1-0541307	–	Generator: 9N, 3Li/REF, 160 watt–2500L, on some models.
21.12.53	1-0575417	695282	Generator: 160 watt (all types). Formerly 130 watt. Instrument illumination automatic and can be regulated, combined with exterior light switch. Formerly non-adjustable toggle switch. Interior light: door-contact and three settings. Formerly manual switches for interior and instrument panel lights. Windscreen wiper: flat arms; blades of 'Christmas tree' cross-section; Metallic paint. Formerly chrome finished. V-belt: narrower, with synthetic fibre insert. Spare discontinued from tool kit. Ignition and starter lock: combination lock; push button for starter discontinued. Distributor: new type with vacuum control (passenger cars only). Battery clamp strap: new type with over-centre catch. Formerly secured with springs. Door and ignition lock now same type. Formerly two different locks.

1954

The new Beetle 'fulfils the requirement of all sporty VW-drivers'. The engine output is increased from 25 to 30 bhp, that is by 20 per cent (production begins on 21 December 1953). The top speed is thereby raised to 68 mph (110 km/h).

The increased performance is achieved by raising the engine capacity from 1331 cc to 1192 cc and the compression ratio from 5.8 to 6.1 (in August of the same year to 6.6). In addition there are larger inlet valves (from 28 to 30 mm) and improved-flow inlet and exhaust ports. All Beetle engines are fitted with an oil-bath air filter.

The carburettor is fitted with a vacuum take-off, so that the higher performance engine can be equipped with a distributor controlled by vacuum advance. Increased electrical current is provided by raising the generator capacity from 130 to 160 watts.

In the place of the previous ignition lock, a combined starter ignition lock is installed. The push button starter is discontinued.

The rear seat rest is held up by a hook and rubber strap. This stops the backrest falling forward when the brakes are slammed on.

The distribution of the heating air is modified. Air is now emitted only through two enlarged outlets in the front footwell and through the defroster jets in the windscreen surround inside the car. The operating handle for the heater no longer carries an inscription.

The interior light on the Standard saloon is now operated only by a switch built into the light, the Export saloon is fitted with a door contact switch. The battery has a quickly-detachable lid (previously screwed on), which can be removed without recourse to tools. The superior quality of the V-belt makes the provision of a spare V-belt on a new Beetle superfluous.

The windscreen wiper arms apply more pressure (flat profile, previously round profile) and the rubber blades have a 'Christmas tree' cross-section. This is to achieve a smooth sweep and an improved wiping effect. The wiper arms are no longer chromed, but are sprayed with a metallic finish.

Taken as a yearly average, 769 Beetles are produced daily. Volkswagen pays its workers at the end of the year 2.25 DM per hour. The standard VW now costs 3950 DM, the Export model 4850 DM and the Cabriolet 6500 DM. On 10/11 July on the Killeburg in Stuttgart, 18,000 VW drivers with 4,800 *Jubiläums* Volkswagens come together for the second meeting of the *Hunderttausender* (open to any VW that has achieved 100,000 km on one engine). VW chief Nordhoff announces: 'We are still convinced – that I will say it over and over again, since again and again absolutely senseless and unfounded rumours arise of a new Volkswagen – that the blessing lies not in bolder and more magnificent new designs, but in the consistent and tireless redevelopment of every tiny detail until perfection is achieved, which is the mark of a really outstanding car and which brings truly astonishing success. Does anyone seriously believe that we would give up a vehicle type, which has for years brought us such success and so undisputedly holds the number one position in the whole of the European car industry, such that in the USA, where they certainly know their cars, it is recognised as the symbol of the German recovery? We sell the Volkswagen especially in those countries with a large, competitive and from our side highly respected car industry, with one single argument only: Quality!'

Dates and facts

1954	The turnover of the concern exceeds one billion DM for the first time. From now on a yearly 'success' bonus is paid to the workforce.
9.10.	The 100,000th Volkswagen leaves the factory in Wolfsburg. The plan to build its own Transporter factory in Hanover-Stöcken is officially announced.
1.11.	Outside the German boundaries the country with the most Volkswagens on its roads is Belgium with 53,000 vehicles.

New Beetle engine of 1.2-litre capacity and 30 bhp output. A vacuum advance is fitted to the distributor. For better heating of the inlet manifold there is a heating jacket in the centre of the pre-heating pipe.

Spray-painted wind-screen wiper arms with broad sweep. The wiper blades have a 'Christmas tree' cross-section. Optional passenger grab-handle.

Typical interior fittings and upholstery from 1954.

The heating air flows now only through two enlarged openings in the front footwell and through defroster jets in the dashboard inside the car. In place of the previous ignition lock, a combined ignition/starter lock is installed. The dashboard lighting switches on automatically when the external lights are switched on.

Battery strap with quick-action over-centre catch, so that the battery can be removed without tools.

Above left: the reservoir for the brake master cylinder is located in the front luggage bay behind the spare wheel.

Centre: promotion for the engine with an extra 5 'horses'.

Beetle Cabrio: synthetic resin paintwork replaces the cellulose type paint previously standard on this model.

1954   The most important modifications

Year	Chassis No.	Assembly No.	Modification
Engine/clutch/heating			
22.1.54	1-0 591 433	514 590	Dip-stick: Integral loop handle and cap.
6.2.54	1-0 518 795	723 005	Oil cooler marking (month and year) on the underside.
22.3.54	Industrial engine	122-02857	Starting crank: a) gauge of tubing increased from 2 mm to 3 mm. b) seamless tube.
21.4.54	1-0 637 872	770 850	Distributor VJU 4BR 3 mk: improved springs for bob-weights.
17.5.54	1-0 653 400	from 788196 to 794174 from 806314 to 811940	Carburettor 28PCI: nylon float (number 11604). Marking: blue spot.
1.7.54	1-0 678 201	819 078	Oil filler cap: filter mesh discontinued.
19.8.54	1-0 696 501	–	Spare V-belt discontinued in toolkit.
31.8.54	1-0 702 742	–	Piston: 77 mm, flat piston, compression 6.6:1. Inception of the 30 bhp engine.
Bodywork			
25.5.54	1-0 652 823	17 850	VW Cabriolet: synthetic resin finish. Formerly cellulose. Driving mirror with two sun visors, grab-handle for passenger, twin arm rests in the rear stoneguards, tailpipe trim, smooth seats/hood cover, front edge of seat raised, new upholstery.
13.10.54	1-0 730 023	–	Windscreen now shatterproof with clear view area in front of the driver.
10.12.54	1-0 770 501	687 285	Door hinge: instead of previous oil hole, now oil slot for hinge pin lubrication.
Electrics			
31.8.54	1-0 702 742	122 05091	Distributor: VJU 4 BR 8 and VJ BR 8. Rotor arm with groove for dust protection cap.
1.10.54	1-0 722 916	–	Brake tail light housing: lens for brake light discontinued. New double filament bulbs for USA, Canada, Guam.
18.10.54	1-0 734 000	–	Brake tail light housing with water drainage hole underneath.

1955

On 5 August 1955 another production milestone was reached, with 140,000 people taking part in Wolfsburg's '1 Million Volkswagens' celebration. Nordhoff ices the cake with a price cut: the Standard costs 3790 DM, the Export 4700 DM and the Cabriolet 5990 DM.

The optically improved brake tail light and reflector units are raised 60 mm on the rear wings. The brake light lenses on top are discontinued. The lens surfaces are consequently enlarged. Reflectors are added to make the brake lights more noticeable. The lights are equipped with twin filament bulbs. One filament serves as a tail light, the second as a brake light.

A new single-chamber exhaust box with two silenced outlet pipes gives the engine a more pleasant exhaust sound. The exhaust pipes on the Export model are chrome-finished, and on the Standard model sprayed black. The pipes are situated 38 mm and the exhaust box itself 18 mm higher than before, and thereby allow the car to be driven over higher obstacles. With the introduction of the new exhaust box, the induction heating is improved.

A breather/filler assembly bolted onto the engine replaces the previous filler, which had to be removed to top-up the oil. The cover for the filler opening has a bayonet type cap.

The generator pulley is now secured with a smaller nut, which can be loosened with the spark plug spanner. The ring spanner is discontinued from the tool kit.

To create more luggage space in the front luggage bay the upper part of the petrol tank is designed significantly smaller. The luggage space is increased from 70 to 85 litres. The tank capacity (40 litres as before) is maintained by enlargement of the lower part of the tank.

The steering wheel, with new easy to grip rim, is safer and more pleasant to handle. On the Export model the view of the speedo-dial is improved by the use of smaller steering wheel hub and deeper set spokes. The hub and spokes have a new shape.

The rotary knob for the heater is now located in front of the front seats, where it is more easily accessible for the driver. The new gear stick is cranked. In order not to hinder access to the heater knob, the gear lever housing is moved a little further forward.

On the Export model the cables for the handbrake are fixed directly to the handbrake lever. They can be adjusted easily by pushing back the rubber boot.

The front seats are widened by 30 mm and have a more comfortable shape. On the Export model they move on slide rails, which rise at the front. On the Export model the backrests on the front seats are adjustable to three different positions.

To prevent the doors being forced from outside, the quarter-lights are better secured. The catch is now hook-shaped and engages under a projection in the window channel. It is therefore impossible to lift out the locked window by pulling it upwards. The inside door handle is pulled back to open the door, and pushed forward to lock it. The doors have a specially secure lock.

The door and side-panels of the Export model have a leatherette strip at the top, which is divided from the upholstery covered panelling by a wider trim strip.

US Beetles are equipped with reinforced bumpers (Ram-bumpers).

279,986 Beetles leave the factory in Wolfsburg this year – 87,520 more than in the previous year. The Beetle is exported in the meantime to over 100 countries. Particularly successful are the sales in the USA, where a total of 35,581 cars, four times as many as the previous year, is sold. This makes America the most important foreign customer for the VW company.

Dates and facts

1955	1.3.	In Hanover-Stöcken construction begins of the Transporter factory.
	14.5.	General Director Dr Ing e.h. Heinz Nordhoff is made Honorary Professor of the Technischen Hochschule (Technical College) in Brunswick.

Dates and facts

20.6.	The 10,000th Volkswagen industrial engine leaves the assembly line.
14.7.	Karmann in Osnabrück presents the Karmann Ghia coupé to the public. It is priced at 7500 DM. Production is scheduled to begin in August.
5.8.	The 1,000,000th Volkswagen rolls off the line! In recognition of this Prof. Dr Nordhoff is made a freeman of the city of Wolfsburg.
27.10.	In Englewood Cliffs, N.J. Volkswagen of America, Inc. is founded as a trading company, as the custodian and supplier of the American VW market.

Taken as a yearly average, the daily production of the Volkswagen exceeds 1,000 vehicles for the first time.

The top-mounted brake light lenses are dropped from the light assemblies. The brake/tail and reflector units are attached 60 mm higher on the wings. The exhaust box has twin tailpipes. On the Export model they are chrome finished, on the Standard model sprayed black.

Steering wheel with new, easy-grip rim. The Export model has a smaller hub and deeper set spokes, thereby improving the view of the instruments.

The gear stick is cranked. Door and side panelling on the Export model has leatherette protective strips and broader trim. The interior door handle is pulled backwards to open the door.

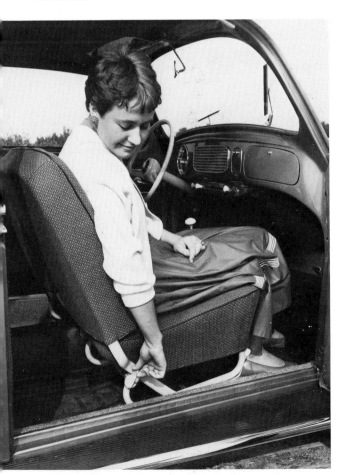

The jack is now to hand beside the spare wheel, fastened to the car body by a bracket with a snap-on clip. The new tank shape increases the luggage space.

Left: front seats are widened by 30 mm and more comfortably designed. On the Export model slide rails for seats rise at the front end. The back-rests can be adjusted to three different angles.

For some Export
countries (USA, Canada,
Guam) the Beetle is
fitted with flashing indicators in the front wings
in place of the sema-
phore arms in the side
panels.

Beetle Cabrio 1956.

On 14.7 1955 Karmann
presents the Karmann
Ghia coupé based on
the VW Beetle.

50

1955 The most important modifications

Year	Chassis No.	Assembly No.	Modification
Engine/clutch/heating			
4.8.55	1-0 929 746	–	Exhaust silencer: now single-chamber box with twin tail pipes, connecting pipe for induction pipe heating.
4.8.55	1-0 929 746	–	Hollow screw: with needle bearing. Cylinder head: instead of the previous 175T1 spark plugs, spark plugs now 225T1s.
Fuel System			
4.8.55	1-0 929 746	5	Fuel tap: without mesh filter, switch position changed.
4.8.55	1-0 929 746	5	Petrol tank: moved and changed in shape. Filler opening 60 mm. Formerly 80 mm. Well for fuel tap.
Front axle/steering			
9.1.55 19.1.55	from 1-0 787 449 to 1-0 797 357	801 042	Steering tie-rod: on approximately 1000 VW saloon/Standard models; steering without lubrication nipple.
11.5.55	1-0 881 293	– 551 576 (Stand.)	Gear lever: Standard and synchromesh models have identical gear lever assembly.
4.8.55	1-0 929 746		Steering wheel: changed in shape, spokes set deeper.
4.8.55	1-0 929 746	–	Torsion bar setting 12° + 30′. Formerly 13° ± 30′
Brakes/wheels/tyres			
4.8.55	1-0 929 746	–	Handbrake cable: bolted to the handbrake lever. Formerly on the actuating arm. (Export model only).
Chassis			
4.8.55	1-0 929 746	–	Gearlever cranked; straight lower section.
23.8.55	1-0 948 000	–	Gear lever: straight, spring and ball below.

Year	Chassis No.	Assembly No.	Modification

Bodywork

4.8.55	1-0 929 746	–	Heating outlet: rotary knob in front of front seats. Formerly behind them. Front seats 30 mm wider. Front seat backrests adjustable to 3 different angles, Export only. Paintwork: Nile Beige, Jungle Green, Reed Green, Polar Silver. Continuing colours: Black, Strato Silver, Jupiter Grey (Standard). Formerly Texas Brown. Seat rails: number of adjustment notches raised from 2 to 7. Luggage bay size increased at front to 85 litres. Formerly 70 litres. At rear 120 litres. Formerly 130 litres. Bonnet, at front: lock and lid support improved, release knob for bonnet moved further to left at front. US Beetle with ram bumpers. Interior fittings: now door and side panels with leatherette strip and trim. Now plastic grab straps. Formerly cloth straps. Chassis tunnel now has rubber covering as standard (Export). (Standard model at front only on chassis tunnel).
4.8.55	1-0 929 746	–	VW Cabriolet: colour, Inca Red.

Electrics

1.4.55	1-0 847 967	–	Flashing indicator lamps for USA, Canada, Guam as optional extra. Formerly: semaphore arms.
19.4.55	1-0 860 576	–	Number plate light: lens and light casing modified for USA, Canada, Guam.
11.6.55	1-0 904 566	–	Ignition/starter switch: lock number on fixing lug.
14.7.55	1-0 927 373	K 826 637	Number plate light: K6V/10 watts. Formerly: L6V/5 watts.
4.8.55	1-0 929 746	–	Battery 66 Ah. Formerly 70 Ah. Brake/tail lights 60 mm higher. Separate brake light lens discontinued. Double filament lamp 5/20 watt. Spark plugs 225T1. Formerly 175T1.

General Modifications

4.8.55	1-0 929 746	–	Tool kit: spark plug spanner used also for 21 mm generator pulley nut. Formerly 36 mm ring spanner (discontinued).
11.8.55	1-0 906 481	M 1092 791	Karmann Ghia coupé: production begins.

1956

There are no changes to the bodywork for this year's model. The 1956 Beetle is fitted with an external rear view mirror on the left-hand side of the vehicle. The Beetle still retains the decidedly sluggish semaphore indicator arms instead of flashing indicator lights. In June, for the first time, 800 Beetles are fitted with tubeless tyres, a little later all Beetles have this new feature. To keep the oil intake in the crankcase clear of sludge and water, the oil intake pipe is shortened somewhat.

The VW motif in the hub caps, formerly in various colours, is from now on sprayed black only.

To improve soundproofing and protection against damp, the padding in the engine bay is reinforced.

So that the Beetle engine starts more easily, the rating of the starter is increased. Besides this, all VW models are fitted with a more powerful windscreen wiper motor with permanent magnetic brake, giving an increased wiping rate.

The Suez crisis has a negative effect on international vehicle production. Despite this, the German car industry can still boast a fine record even in this year. VW increases total turnover by 20 per cent this year (including Transporters) to 395,690 vehicles. The combined workforce in Volkswagen factories grows by 4102 to 35,672 employees.

Dates and facts

1956	20.2.	The 500,000th Volkswagen for Export leaves the Wolfsburg factory, destination Stockholm.
	8.3.	In Hanover-Stöcken the first Volkswagen Transporter rolls off the line. The next day the first vehicles completed there are delivered to the dealers.
	8.3.	VW acquires shares in the South African VW Import Company and founds a subsidiary assembly plant in South Africa.

Rubber-based hair matting in the front seats lengthened by 15 mm.

Typical upholstery design for 1956.

54

1956   The most important modifications

Year	Chassis No.	Assembly No.	Modification
Engine/clutch/heating			
5.6.56	1 210 230	1 477 496	Vacuum pipe. Now underneath accelerator cable. Formerly above the choke cable.
21.8.56	1 266 678	1518 878	Camshaft timing gear. Now in light alloy, all export Saloons. Formerly: Resitex.
Brakes/wheels/tyres			
30.6.56	1 232 835	–	Tubeless tyres fitted to 800 vehicles of various models.
10.7.56	1 239 921/141		Tubeless tyres, 5.60 − 15, on all models.
11.7.56	1 245 207/151		
13.7.56	1 248 030/111 + 113		
Bodywork			
May 56	1 158 165	–	Karmann Ghia coupé: front and rear bumpers 3-section, hollow overriders with mounting brackets.
6.8.56	1 252 386	–	Colour: Agave for VW Export Saloon.
8.8.56	1 257 230	–	Door lock: new lock plate with adjustable wedge on some models. Formerly non-adjustable.
6.9.56	1 283 328	32 065	VW Cabriolet: brass pins and studs for hood fastening. Formerly: steel pins and studs.
4.9.56	–	–	Hub caps: VW emblem now only in black.
19.10.56	1 329 017	–	External mirror for all cars (home market).
23.10.56	1 326 040	32 880	Door hinges (151): lubrication nipple discontinued.
3.4.56	1 149 147	–	Colours: new, Prairie Beige, Coral Red, Horizon Blue, Diamond Green. Continued lines: Black and Polar Silver.
3.4.56	1 149 147		Front seats: rubber/hair internal padding made 15 mm longer.
1.12.56	VW Cabriolet		New colours: Pearl Blue and Bamboo. Iris Blue and Sepia Silver discontinued.
Electrics			
22.2.56	1113 449	M.1333 500	Distributor: Centrifugal and vacuum curve set from 3° to 5° lower in upper engine speed range.

Year	Chassis No.	No.	Modification
22.6.56	1 227 367	–	Semaphore arms on Inca Red Cabriolet, with yellow and reddish tint.
14.8.56	1 261 493	M.1510 980	Ignition coil: TE6 B1 (greater ignition performance). Formerly TE6 A3.
20.8.56	–	–	Semaphore arms, Inca Red Cabriolet: now only yellowish colouring. Formerly reddish colouring also.
10.10.56	1 320 559	HA 958 55	Starter: EED 0.5/6L4/0.5 HP. 4 commutator brushes.

General modifications

March 56	–	–	Ground clearance 155 mm (VW Export saloon). Formerly 172 mm.

1957

The windscreen and the rear window are considerably enlarged this year. The enlargement of the windscreen is made at the top and the sides, the window pillars being made narrower. The area of the rear window also is extended in width and in height.

The new dashboard, with the speedometer retaining the same design, has the control knobs differently arranged; on the right is a significantly broader glove compartment, and a pull-ashtray in the centre of the car with easier access. To avoid confusion, light and windscreen wiper switches are placed quite a distance apart. The ignition lock has been moved closer to the driver. On the Export model a moulding strip runs across the whole width of the dashboard. The side panelling in the interior is now totally covered with synthetic material.

The engine cover has a new shape for easier mounting and illumination of a two line numberplate. On the engine cover of the Cabriolet the air louvres run horizontally.

To improve the operation of the accelerator, the customary Beetle accelerator roller is replaced by a flat pedal.

At the International Automobile Show in Frankfurt Karmann presents the two-seater Ghia Cabriolet (production begins 1 August). It costs 8250 DM.

At the end of November the 40,000th employee is taken on. The annual turnover of Volkswagen exceeds 2 billion DM for the first time, of which proceeds from Exports make up 52.5 per cent. Daily production on an average for the year increases to 2141 vehicles (including Transporters). A total of 380,561 private cars is built.

Dates and facts

1957	1.1.	Sweden receives its 100,000th Volkswagen.
	19.9.	In Osnabrück the Karmann assembly plant presents the new two-seater Cabriolet on the VW Chassis, which is to cost 8250 DM.
	1.11.	Volkswagen takes over the Henschel works in Kassel-Altenbauna.
		The 300,000th Transporter leaves the Assembly line in Hanover.
	15.11.	Holland gets its 100,000th Volkswagen.
	6.12.	In Melbourne Volkswagen (Australasia) Pty Ltd is formed with a nominal capital of 250,000 Aust. Pounds. The capital is later to be increased to 5 million Aust. Pounds. VW GmbH has a 51 per cent share. The new subsidiary is to take on the manufacture of Volkswagens with a limited German supply of parts.
	28.12.	The 2,000,000 Volkswagen leaves the production line.

The Beetle with larger windscreen and rear window.

The area of the rear window is 95 per cent larger than its predecessor.

The windscreen is enlarged at the top and at the sides. The surface area is thereby increased by 17 per cent. As a result of the larger rear window a larger driving mirror is fitted.

Completely new dashboard. The ashtray is located underneath. The glove compartment is 50 per cent wider, and the lid springs open automatically when the button is pressed. The loudspeaker for the radio is located to the left of the speedometer. The ignition starter lock is moved from the passenger area and is now located in direct proximity to the steering column. Light and windscreen windscreen wiper switches are placed far apart. All control knobs are newly designed.

The accelerator takes the form of a rubber covered flat pedal on all models. On the Export and Cabriolet models a moulding strip runs the whole length of the dashboard. The side panel trim is entirely plastic. The floor is covered with grey rubber matting.

Cross-section of the Beetle with enlarged windscreen and rear window.

Left: Beetle Cabrio: windscreen enlarged by 8 per cent and rear window by 45 per cent. Narrower pillars. The louvres in the rear cover are arranged horizontally.

1957   The most important modifications

Year	Chassis No.	Assembly No.	Modification
Engine/clutch/heating			
9.1.57	1394 163	34 347 (151)	Heating: Heating duct in body sills. Heating outlets in front footwell moved back. Side panelling modified accordingly.
1.8.57	1 600 440	–	Oil-bath air filter: shape changed. Higher, smaller in external diameter.
Fuel system			
1.8.57	1 600 440	–	Fuel consumption: reduced from previous 7.5 l/100 km average consumption, according to DIN 70030, to about 7.3/100 km.
Dec 57			Carburettor 29 PCI: altitude correction as service part.
Front axle/steering			
7.6.57	1 568 040 (111)	–	Steering-wheel: splined shaft formerly 24 splines, now 48 splines.
16.9.57	1 649 253	22 922	Steering wheel (143). Steering wheel with deeper set boss and semi-circular horn ring. Steering column shortened.
20.12.57	1 769 756	1 781 718	Tie rods available with maintenance-free joints. (20,000 vehicles, optionally.)
Chassis			
1.8.57	1 600 440	–	Accelerator pedal: now rubber-covered oblong pedal. Formerly pedal with roller.
Bodywork			
1.8.57	1 600 440	–	Cool air inlet: modified openings and better drainage. Engine cover: better waterproofing and modified number plate light. Cabrio: cooling air louvres horizontal instead of vertical; water trap inside and drainage pipe.
			Windscreen enlarged at top and at both sides. Rear window enlarged at top and at sides. Painwork: Colours Light Bronze, Diamond Grey, Fern Blue and Capri. Continued lines: Black, Coral Red and Agave. Painwork (151): colours Alabas-

Year	Chassis No.	No.	Modification
			ter and Atlas Blue. Continued lines: Black, Shetland Grey, Inca Red and Bamboo.
16.9.57	1649 253	22 292 (143)	Paintwork: colours Aero Silver and Cardinal Red. Continued lines: Bamboo, Brilliant Red, Cognac, Dolphin Blue and Toucan Black. Defroster outlet: underneath rear window inside.
			Sound proofing: 12 mm thick glass wool layer between rear wall of engine bay and soundproofing cardboard. Impregnated felt insert soundproof covering on rear wheel arches. Seats: Adjustment cams for three different seating positions.

Electrics

Year	Chassis No.	No.	Modification
1.2.57	1 423 927		New windscreen wiper motor with permanent magnetic brake. Number plate light: fixed higher with diffusing lens. 5 watt spherical bulb; improved illumination for number plate.
1.8.57	1 600	–	Windscreen wipers: wiper arms brought closer together. Longer wiper blades. Broader sweep.
16.9.57	1 649 253	(143) 22 922	Fuel gauge now on dashboard between speedometer and clock; sender unit in fuel tank. Indicator switch with automatic return, combined with headlight flasher.
16.10.57	1 676 789	(143) 24 203	Number plate light: spherical bulbs. Formerly festoon bulbs.
19.10.57	1 708 050	(143) 24 781	Brake indicator lights: spherical bulbs. Formerly festoon bulbs.
1.11.57	1 709 421	–	Battery: acid level 5 mm over top of plates or exactly to acid-level mark. Formerly 10-15 mm.

General Modifications

Year	Chassis No.	No.	Modification
1.8.57	1 626 393	–	Karmann Ghia Cabriolet (141): production begins of two-seater, in the colours Toucan Black, Pearl White, Diamond Grey, Colorado, Amazon, Graphite Silver, Bernina. Hood: black or bright grey, brown, beige, bright green, bright grey and blue.

1958

The Beetle for the home market gets an enlarged exterior mirror; the size across flats of the mudguard bolts is reduced from 14 to 13 mm. In order to trap the metallic swarf in the engine, the engines are fitted with a magnetic oil drain plug. A socket is put in the jack to take the operating arm, thus making jack operation easier.

The Karmann Ghia models for the US market are fitted with reinforced bumpers.

While automobile production in America sinks by 29.1 per cent, in Europe it can be considerably increased. The growth rate in the Federal Republic is 23.3 per cent. 1,495,256 vehicles are manufactured this year.

The VW share of that figure is 37 per cent, or 553,399 vehicles (451, 526 private cars). At the year end, daily production runs at 2,400 Volkswagens.

On the occasion of the presentation of the Elmer A Sperry Prize to Prof. Dr Nordhoff, Prof. Dr Porsche and the Volkswagen workforce, the VW General Director gives a speech in New York, in which he stresses: "I am far more attracted to the idea of offering people something of genuine value, a high-quality product with a low purchase price and an incomparable resale value, than to be continually pestered by a mob of hysterical stylists who try to sell people something which they really don't want to buy at all. I don't think any differently today: consistent improvement in quality and value without a rise in price; higher wages, better living and working conditions, without making the customer pay for them; simplification and intensifying of the garage and spares network; the building of a product, of which I and every other member of the workforce can be truly proud".

Dates and facts

1958	13.6.	The 250,000th VW exchange engine is completed. Production began of these engines on 5 November 1948. One in every ten Volkswagens runs on a replacement engine in this year. The price of this item is 495 DM, and gives a saving of 58 per cent compared to a new engine.
	30.6.	Austria get its 50,000th Volkswagen.
	1.7.	Spare parts factory in Kassel goes into production.
	16.10.	The 400,000th VW Transporter is manufactured.
	1.11.	From now on, besides the VW Transporter, all VW engines also are produced in the Hanover factory.

1958   The most important modifications

Year	Chassis No.	Assembly No.	Modification
Engine/clutch/heating			
20.3.58	1 882 550	–	Spark plug spanner: formerly with retaining spring, now with rubber sleeve.
5.6.58	1 975 105	2 385 613	Carburettor 28 PCI: plastic venturi tube (as standard). Formerly light alloy.
Front-axle/steering			
29.4.58	1 925 488	1944 448	Steering swivel pin bush now bronze, rolled and slit lengthways. Formerly Main-metal.
Rear axle/transmission			
9.1.58	1 789 807	1503 797	Magnetic oil drain plug: all VW Export/Saloons have magnetic oil drain plug.
Bodywork			
3.1.58	1 764 743	(143/141) 27 435	Bumpers with impact protection front and rear (USA).
7.1.58	1 786 160	–	Wheel paintwork on Cabriolet, Ghia Coupé and Ghia Cabriolet sprayed Pearl White (for 10 colour combinations).
15.1.58	1 788 180	(143) 28 198	Demister jet for rear window now with control flap.
10.2.58	1 816 990	(151) 43 331	Interior fittings: coat hooks.
14.4.58	1 904 235	–	Mudguard bolts: 13 mm bolts for mudguard/bodywork, mud-guard/running board and horn fastening.
19.9.58	2 071 106	–	Front compartment lid: cable pull handle moved closer to steering column.
Electrics			
30.6.58	1 994 320	2 425 147	Distributor rotor and spark plug caps remotely suppressed.

1959

Improvements this year are mainly of the technical kind. The bodywork remains the same as before. The new model year can be identified by the fixed door handles with press buttons.

The engine/transaxle assembly is tipped forward two degrees, enabling the swing axle pivot point to be lowered by 15 mm. An anti-roll bar is added to the front axle. The rear suspension is more responsive; it is more progressive now at higher loadings. All these new measures go to improve the handling. The two-spoke steering wheel has a deeper-set hub and a semi-circular horn ring. The indicator arm is self-cancelling. An upholstered sun visor replaces the old transparent plastic sun visor with alloy frame on the export model. The passenger door of the export model now has an arm rest with an open centre for use as a door-pull.

Under the rear seats two plastic-covered vertical panels are inserted for sound-proofing. These panels, or heel-boards, block off the two openings under the rear seat. The panel in front of the battery has a loop-strap for easy removal.

Indicator arm action is quietened further by the addition of rubber stops.

Production rises this year by 25.9 per cent. VW manufacture a total of 557,407 private cars, of which 58 per cent are exported. The standard Beetle now has only a 5.1 per cent share of the private car market.

The company turnover passes the 3 billion DM level for the first time (3.5 billion precisely).

The workforce totals 54,120. 2,839 Volkswagens are produced daily.

Dates and facts

1959	21.8	In the Hanover-Stöcken factory the 50,000th VW employee is taken on.
	25.8	The 3,000,000th Volkswagen comes off the line in Wolfsburg, and in Hanover-Stöcken the 500,000th Volkswagen Transporter.

Export model:
Two-spoke steering
wheel with deeper-set
hub. The horn is
operated by a
semi-circular ring.
Indicator lever cancels
automatically.
Upholstered sun visor.

Two vertical partition
panels under the rear
seat, called
Fersenbretter
[heelboards].

Footrest for the
passenger. Front-seat
backrests more steeply
angled and with a
deeper curve.

Arm rest for the passenger with an open centre for use as a grip.

Fixed door-handle. Door lock opened by pressing button.

Front axle fitted with anti-roll bar on all models.

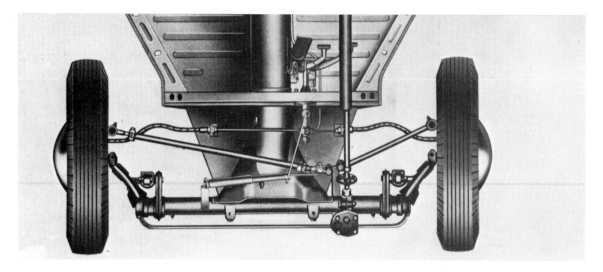

1959 The most important modifications

Year	Chassis No.	Item No.	Modification
Engine/clutch/heating			
4.5.59	2 409 056	2 939 201	Heating: heat exchangers and operating gear modified.
13.5.59	2 425 182	2 957 823	Silencer/heat exchanger and silencer/tailpipe joints now have conical asbestos rings and clamps.
13.5.59	2 428 094	2 958 225	Silencer stub pipes shortened by 10 mm
3.7.59	2 503 092	3 052 042	V-belt: heat-resistant V-belt as standard part; 5-8 belt adjustment pulley spacers. Formerly 8-11 spacers.
6.8.59	2 528 668	3 072 724	Dipstick: measurement from the lower end of the dipstick to the oil level mark is 40 mm. Formerly 44 mm. Oil drain plug: in sump plate. Formerly in crankcase.
Fuel system			
29.1.59	2 269 017	–	Fuel tank: cap 80 mm diameter with ventilation via seal. Formerly labyrinth ventilation.
23.2.59	2 303 769	2 816 496	Carburettor 28 PCI: with double vacuum unit and a distributor with vacuum advance only (5000 engines, option).
6.8.59	2 533 139 (143)	–	Carburettor 28 PCI: modified and with vacuum advance only distributor installed. All models.
5.11.59	2 708 099	–	Fuel tap, cork seal. Formerly Thiokol.
Front axle/steering			
22.1.59	2 256 907	2 278 029	Steering tie rod (right-hand drive): length of left tie rod 807 mm formerly 814 mm. Length of right tie rod 325 mm, formerly 318 mm.
6.8.59	2 528 668 (113)	–	Steering wheel: two-spoke steering wheel with deep-set hub. Steering column with ball bearing mounted in outer tube.
6.8.59	2 533 099 (151)	–	
6.8.59	2 533 139 (143)	–	
6.8.59	2 533 158 (141)	–	
7.10.59	2 648 938	2 668 581	Link pins: hex socket 8 mm for adjustment. Formerly flush at both ends.

Year	Chassis No.	Assembly No.	Modification
Brakes/wheels/tyres			
12.1.59	2 245 160	–	Hub cap removing hook in tool-kit.
Bodywork			
19.1.59	2 252 455 (131)	–	Sun visor: new padded design. Formerly from transparent plastic.
20.1.59	2 251 316 (143)	–	
22.1.59	2 252 685 (151)	–	
26.1.59	2 257 235 (141)	–	Dashboard: now with covering and padded edge.
26.1.59	2 257 980 (141)	–	Hood: studded trim on front of hood discontinued. Hood covering and front of hood modified; sealing modified.
26.1.59	2 261 050 (141/143)	–	Grab-handle for passenger now more flexible design.
6.7.59	2 490 635 (143)	–	Dashboard-cover: new shutters for heating outlets, and lower retaining strip.
6.7.59	2 490 960 (141)	–	
10.3.59	2 317 671 (151)	–	Rear seat springing modified. Padding raised and softer.
6.8.59	2 528 668	–	Paintwork (VW Export): Jade Green, Mango Green, Ceramic Green, Pebble Grey, Arctic, Indigo Blue and India Red. Continued lines: black. Formerly Reseda Green, Kalahari Beige, Fjord Blue, Granite Red, Capri and Diamond Grey. Paintwork (VW Cabriolet): jade green, Sargasso green, slate grey, rock grey and paprika. Continued lines: black and alabaster. Formerly atlas blue, Inca red, Shetland grey and bamboo.
	2 533 099 (151)	–	
	2 533 139 (143)	–	
	2 533 158 (141)	–	
6.8.59	2 528 668	–	Exterior door handles: more rigid construction with push button operation. Formerly pull handles. Door-lock and striker plate modified and requiring less closing pressure. Arm rest on right with recess for gripping. Front seats: inclined towards doors. Side windows at rear (143) pivot opening. Right-hand drive: new Type 144 and 142.
6.8.59	2 528 668 (141)	–	Hood: new rear section with replaceable window.

Year	Chassis No.	Assembly No.	Modification
6.8.59	2 533 139 (143) 2 533 158 (141)		Arm rest on right with recess for gripping. Front seat backrest: curved design. Sun visor: padded design. Floor coverings: two-piece design. Formerly five separate mats. Foot rest on passenger side. Closing panels (heel boards) for the openings underneath the rear seat. Soundproofing: Floorpan with bitumen-felt overlay. Muffling felt on wheel arches, luggage bay floor and around the rear window. Mudguard, at front: bracket for headlight shell dropped. Hole above for cable with rubber boot.
11.8.59	2 539 142	–	Trim mouldings now sealed with rubber caps from outside. Formerly with rubber caps fixed on inside of body panel.
29.8.59	2 575 176	–	Catch for quarter-light: new reinforced design. Inner web of bearing slot reinforced. Quarter-light frame modified.
9.9.59	2 577 839 (151)	–	Doors: door buffer fitted under door catch.
14.9.59	2.600 263 (151)	–	Front bonnet: nickel-silver soldered between lid support and gutter.
24.9.59	2 616 071 (151)	–	Sound proofing: felt matting on floor of luggage bay under rear window.

Electrics

Year	Chassis No.	Assembly No.	Modification
6.4.59	2 368 910	–	Spark plugs: now 175. Formerly 225.
6.8.59	2 528 668 (113) 2 533 099 (151)	–	Indicator arm switch: now automatic arm return switch. Dipped beam lights now with fuses in front fusebox. Indicator arm: new rubber quietening stops.
6.8.59	2 528 890	–	Generator 180 watt. Formerly 160 watt.

1960

The Beetle loses its semaphore indicator arms! Instead, indicator lights are mounted on the front mudguards, while the rear indicator lights are combined with the tail and brake lights in one single housing. The relay for the indicator system is located on the rear of the dashboard.

The headlights on all models have asymmetric dip beams. Even when the lights are dipped the nearside of the road remains well lit for a considerable distance.

While this is the extent of the visible exterior modifications of the new model year, under the engine cover a small revolution takes place: after six years of production, the engine performance is raised from 30 to 34 bhp. In its basic construction, the engine resembles the Transporter unit, well-known since May 1959. The higher engine performance is principally achieved by raising the compression ratio (from 6.6 to 7.0:1).

A new carburettor (Solex 28 PICT) is fitted, with automatic choke in place of the hand-operated one. The automatic choke butterfly is electrically controlled, and the distributor has a vacuum take-off from the induction manifold pipe. Running on a cold engine is improved by the injection of warm air to the engine. The warm air is taken from the left-hand heat exchanger and directed via a flexible hose and an intake pipe to the oil-bath air filter of the carburettor.

To increase luggage space significantly, the fuel tank is newly designed. The luggage capacity is thereby increased from 85 to 140 litres. The filler neck (internal diameter 60 mm) is moved to the left-hand side in the process. Venting of the fuel tank no longer takes place through the filler cap, but through a special tube at the filler neck, which runs down the side of the fuel tank and out.

For the brakes a transparent fluid reservoir (plastic) is installed. It is secured under the front bonnet behind the spare wheel by a strap on a bodywork bracing plate.

From now on a sun visor is provided as standard for the passenger, and a grab-handle is fitted in front of the passenger seat. The coat hook above the grab straps on the left and right are now made of plastic for increased safety.

The speedometer now has a range from 0 to 140 km/h. The red marks showing the maximum speeds in 1st, 2nd and 3rd gears are discontinued.

A windscreen washer is now installed in all cars. The pull-pump is combined with the pull-switch for the windscreen wipers. The transparent water tank with about one litre capacity is located under the front bonnet behind the spare wheel.

An eight circuit fuse box is located under the dashboard on the right beside the steering column. The fuses are accessible from inside the car.

The combined ignition/starter lock has a locking device which allows the starter to be operated again only after the ignition has been switched off. Further striking improvements: A full synchromesh 4-speed gearbox; and running board material and wing beading colour co-ordinated with the car's paintwork.

The whole of the German Automobile Industry produces more than 2 million vehicles this year.

VW alone produces 725,939 cars and 139,919 Transporters. The Standard version's share of this represents only 3.4 per cent. Company turnover increases to 4.6 billion DM. At the end of the year there are 1,319 VW agents and 4,088 overseas.

Nordhoff speaks in Düsseldorf at the economic union. "All over the world, wherever Volkswagen is given a fair chance, the public has gone for this car. Even with a daily production of 4,000 we remain months behind demand, even though each month means 80,000 more VW's, a figure never reached before in Europe and exceeded, even in the USA, by only two makes . . . In this way it has been possible to produce the 4 millionth Volkswagen – now we are moving towards the next million.''

Dates and facts

1960	11.3.	Volkswagen France is set up as the marketing company for France.
	27.4.	The 600,000th VW Transporter is produced.
	15.6.	The 500,000th VW is exported to the USA. The millionth visitor since 1949 tours the Wolfsburg works.
	22.8.	Volkswagenwerk GmbH becomes a joint stock company. 40 per cent of the capital remains in the hands of the State and the State of Lower Saxony. 60 per sent is to be sold off to the public.
	25.11.	Decision made to establish the Volkswagen Foundation to promote science and technology in research and training; the aim is for it to be established by April 1961. The foundation derives its funding capital from the proceeds of the sale of 360 million DM worth of VW shares (60 per cent).

Indicators on front mudguards; at the rear they are integrated into the stop- and tail-lights. Asymmetric beam headlamps. The key slot on the door lock barrel is horizontal and protected internally by a flap.

34 bhp engine. Automatic choke Solex 28 PICT carburettor. Choke cable discontinued.

Air cleaner with intake air pre-heating to improve idling and running at low engine speeds.

Export model: passenger grab-handle. Upholstered sun-visor for passenger also. Combined ignition-starter switch with lock-out device for starter.

Speedometer calibrated to 140 km/h.

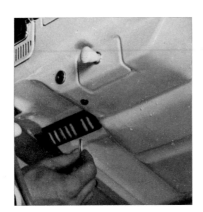

Eight-circuit fuse box next to steering column, accessible from inside the car.

Fuel filler on left-hand side. Diameter of filler neck is 60 mm.

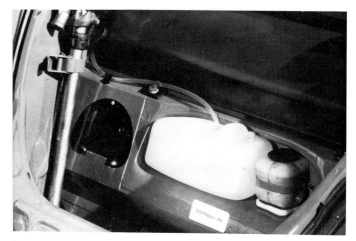

Behind the spare wheel is fitted the transparent brake fluid reservoir and a 1-litre capacity screen washer bottle.

Cross-section of redesigned Beetle. Volume of luggage compartment increased from 85 to 140 litres by redesigned fuel tank.

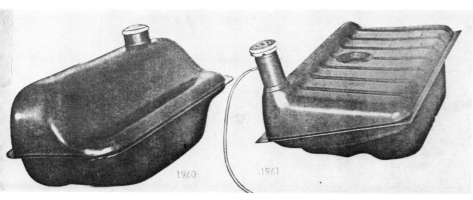

New design of fuel tank allows increase in luggage space.

1960   The most important modifications

Year	Chassis No.	Assembly No.	Modification
Engine/clutch/heating			
7.1.60	–	3351 754	Valve clearance adjusting nut now 13 mm. Formerly 14 mm.
1.8.60	3192507	5000 001	Engine uprated to 34 bhp/1192 cc, compression ratio 7:1. Formerly 30 bhp/1192 cc, compression ratio: 6.1:1. 28 PICT carburettor. Heated inlet air provided by tube to air filter from heat exchanger.
5.8.60	3223145	5042 363	Pre-heater tube: new gasket for left-hand connector flange, hole diameter 6 mm. Formerly 16 mm.
Front axle/steering			
2.3.60	2921552	2926 037	Trailing arm: new outer needle bearing, hardened face. Formerly plastic bush. Steering damper. Located between top axle tube and long tie rod.
Rear axle/gears			
1.8.60	3192507	–	Transaxle: new: one piece casing, synchromesh and needle roller bearings on forward gears. Split driveshaft. Formerly two-piece casing, no synchromesh on first gear, one piece drive-shaft. New: 3rd gear 29:22 teeth, 4th gear 24:27 teeth. Formerly 3rd 28:23, 4th 23:28.
1.8.60	3192507	–	Rear suspension: rubber buffer lengthened by 10 mm.
Bodywork			
16.3.60	2940783 (141) 2940880 (143)	–	Exterior mirror now without plastic frame, allowing greater field of vision.
25.3.60	2960114 (143) 2960127 (141)	– –	Door window: screws for window raiser, guide-rail moved. Better sealing of window cavity.
29.3.60	2967161 (141) 2967166 (151)	– –	Hood: wire sewn into space along hood seam. Roof frame as far as centre pillars.
9.5.60	3 060 711	–	Warm air ducts: plastic duct wth silencer between engine and bodywork. Formerly metal ducts and silencers beneath rear seats.

Year	Chassis No.	No.	Modification
1.8.60	3192507	–	Paintwork (VW export): Black, Pastel Blue, Ruby, Beryl Green, Turquoise, Pearl White, Golf Blue. Formerly: Jade Green, Mango Green, Ceramic Green, Pebble Grey, Arctic, Indigo and India Red.
			Front axle beam mounting: captive threaded bush extended by 7 mm. Mounting bolts moved rearwards.
			Door handles (also Standard model): door handle and lock barrel altered; key slot horizontal, recessed and fitted with dust cover. Three new key types: SC, SU and SV.
			Hood catches (Cabrio): of a different shape and screwed on. Formerly riveted on.
			Bonnet release cable (type 142, 144, 152): Right-hand drive cars with cable pull on right. Formerly cable pull on left.
			Engine cover (type 113/151): revised to accommodate longer engine.
			Engine cover (type 141/143): revised to accommodate longer engine.
			Interior fittings (standard): new driver's sun visor. New adjustable driver's seat backrest.
			Front seats and backrests: springs improved, also frames and upholstery.
			Luggage compartment: front 140 litre capacity. Formerly 85 litres.

Electrics

Year	Chassis No.	No.	Modification
22.1.60 8.2.60	284951 2880160	3262 188 (141/143) 3604 932 (111/113)	Ignition leads: resistor type ignition leads. Formerly spark plug terminals and distributor rotor suppressed.
22.1.60	2849651	3262 188	Distributor: Bosch ZV/PAU R 4R1 with vacuum advance only (Ghia models). Formerly ZV/JUR 4R1.
1.8.60	3192507	–	Oil pressure switch (also Standard model) non-adjustable. Formerly adjustable.
			Brake-light switch (also Standard model): push-on terminal. Formerly screw terminal.
			Dip switch (also Standard model): moved 10 mm further to left.

Year	Chassis No.	No.	Modification
			Fuse box (also Standard model): eight-circuit, transparent fuse box next to steering column. Formerly fuse box behind dashboard.
			Speedometer: range 0-140 km/h without intermediate markings. Formerly, range 0-120 km/h.
			Speedometer cable protective tube (also Standard model) tube discontinued.
			Screen washer unit (also Standard model): washer operation integral with wiper switch. Formerly no washers.
			Ignition/starter switch (also standard model): non-repeat starter switch fitted.
			Door contact switch: earthing by self-tapping screw. Formerly by retaining spring.
			Starter (also Standard model): either Bosch EED 0.5/6L 49, Bosch EEF 0.5/6L 1 20 mm shorter. 'VW' plug connector for terminal 50. Formerly: Bosch EED 0.5/6L 49 'VW'.
			Headlamps (also Standard model): asymmetric dip beam.
19.8.60	3248025	5105 302	Ignition timing: 10 deg before top dead centre. Formerly 7.5 deg before top dead centre.
20.10.60	3390251	5242646	Resistor type ignition leads: orange-red. Deep red continued.
	3390251	3903 620	Formerly carmine red (two designs).
17.11.60	3411658 (143)	–	Indicators, front: yellow lens.
	3411659 (141)	–	Formerly clear.
	3411668 (144)	–	
18.11.60	3411800 (142)	–	

1961

So that the indicator lights could be better seen when the rear lights were switched on, the single unit rear light was replaced by a double section design. Further improvements: the bonnet lid on the export model is spring-loaded; the bonnet support is discontinued. The windscreen washer is changed from hand operation to pneumatic operation. The compressed air can be changed at the petrol station.

To accelerate defrosting of the windscreen, the heating outlets in the footwell can be closed by a sliding cover. Two additional heating outlets are provided in the heel-boards in the rear.

The petrol level, up until now determined by means of the reserve valve, is now indicated on a petrol gauge.

A change in the cam enables the front seat backrests to be adjusted further. Furthermore, longer seat rails allow the seats a greater range of adjustment.

A red line on the speedometer marks the 50 km/h point.

Prices: Export Beetle 4740 DM, Standard Beetle 3790 DM, Beetle Cabriolet 5990 DM, Ghia Coupé 6900 DM, Ghia Cabriolet 7600 DM.

Dates and facts

1961	16.1.	Sale of VW shares until 15.3: issue price 3.5 times per value, less community discount.
	1.7.	First general meeting of the Volkswagen Company held in production hall 9 on the Wolfsburg site.
	1.9.	The new VW 1500 is incorporated into the production programme as a saloon and Karmann Ghia Coupé.
	18.10.	On this day the 11-year long VW saver court case ends with a settlement.
	4.12.	5 million Volkswagens have been built since the end of the war. For the first time the total production of the concern as a whole exceeds one million vehicles in a year.

Dual-section lights on the rear wings.

The bonnet when open is supported by two sprung rods.

Compressed air tank for windscreen washer.

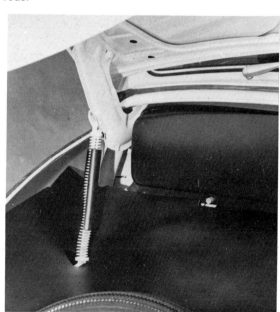

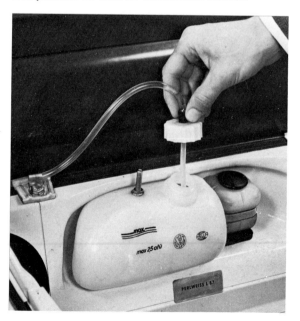

78

Switch for pneumatic windscreen washer.

Heating outlets in the front with sliding covers.

Air outlets in the heel-boards.

Seat belt anchorage points built in on all models.

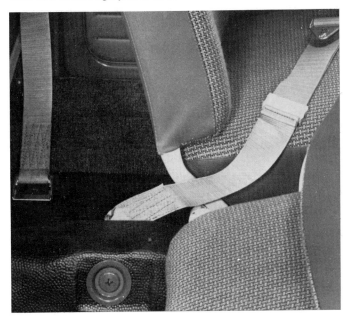

Seat rails lengthened at the back. Back rests can be adjusted further to the rear.

Lubrication nipple in the handbrake cables until August 1961, after that maintenance free.

Upholstery design for 1962.

Starter/ignition lock on the steering column on all models. A petrol gauge replaces the fuel tap.

1961   The most important modifications

Year	Chassis No.	Assembly No.	Modification
Fuel system			
11.5.61	Industrial engine	122-084 781	Carburettor 26VFIS: Equalising air outlet 170 (from carburettor no. 5554995). Formerly 160.
31.7.61	4 010 995	–	Petrol gauge: for export models. Formerly reserve fuel tap.
Front-axle/steering			
30.6.61	3 933 185 (143)	–	Steering: worm-and-roller steering (home and abroad). Formerly worm and peg.
30.6.61	3 933 247 (141)		
30.6.61	3 933 263 (151)	–	
31.7.61	4010 995	–	Steering: worm-and-roller steering, fixed assembly (except standard model, export model home market only). Formerly: spindle steering. Tie-rods: adjustable left and right, apart from standard model (home market only). Formerly: right tie rod only adjustable. Tie-rods now of maintenance-free design (home market only). Formerly with lubrication nipple.
30.8.61	4089 142	4068 130	Tie-rods: adjustable left and right, and maintenance free (foreign market). Formerly: right tie-rod only adjustable, lubrication nipples.
Rear axle/gears			
16.11.61	4289 952	–	Gear stick: conical with smaller head.
Brakes/wheels/tyres			
8.8.61	4036 536	–	Handbrake cables: maintenance-free protective sleeves. Formerly with lubrication nipple.
Bodywork			
16.3.61	3711 714	–	Door lock wedge made from plastic in an injection-moulded housing.
25.3.61	3 712 664 (151)	–	Door seal: lip in latch area about 4 mm wider than previously (on some models from 20.2.61)
28.3.61	3 771 255	–	Front seats: back rests fastened by crankpin with cap nut.

Year	Chassis No.	Assembly No.	Modification
31.7.61	4 010995	–	Heating: outlets in front footwell with sliding shutters (except standard model). Heel-boards with warm air outlets (export model only).
31.7.61	4 010 995	–	Seat belt mountings provided for driver and passenger.
31.7.61	4 010 995		Front seats: seat rails lengthened at the rear. Range of adjustment 120 mm (except standard model). Formerly 100 mm.
31.7.61	4 010 995	–	Doors: new door retainer (except Ghia models). Formerly door stay bar.
31.7.61	4 010 995	–	Bonnet lid: supported in open position by two spring-loaded rods (except standard model).
31.7.61	4 010 995	–	Paintwork (Export model): anthracite. Continued lines: black, ruby, green, turquoise, pearl white and gulf blue. Pastel blue discontinued.
21.8.61	4 057 923	–	Front seat back rests: change in the cam enables further adjustment forwards and backwards (also on driver's seat in standard model).
23.8.61	4 060 506	–	Door retainer: new holding strap with grooved pin.
14.12.61	4 357 893	–	Door hinges: hinge pins phosphated and treated with molybdenum disulphide. Formerly oil lubricated.

Electrics

Year	Chassis No.	Assembly No.	Modification
14.2.61	3672005	5552894	Ignition coil: protective rubber cap for ignition lead discontinued.
2.5.61	3856472	–	Tail brake indicator lights: new dual section design for export and standard models (home).
4.5.61	3862145	–	Speedometer: red mark on dial indicating 50 km/h point. (Only on speedometer with km markings).
29.5.61	3924800	5843201	Oil pressure switch: operating pressure 0.15–0.45 bar. Formerly 0.3–0.6 bar.
30.6.61	3933185 (143)	–	Ignition/starter switch: now
30.6.61	3933347 (141)	–	with non-repeat starter as optional extra (home only).
30.6.61	3933263 (151)	–	Steering/starter lock: available
31.7.61	4010995		for all Volkswagens except Ghia models, as optional extra (home only)

1962

This year sees a wealth of detail improvements. Heating, which until now has been provided by passing air across the hot cylinders, is now provided by heat exchangers. The new ducting system produces an odour-free air supply.

All models are now fitted with hydraulic brakes; the cap for the brake fluid reservoir is now screwed on. The crest is removed from the bonnet lid, and a new VW emblem is fitted at the top of the bonnet. The moulding on the bonnet is increased in length.

The rear outlets for the footwell heating are equipped with a regulating lever. An easy-clean plastic headlining replaces the previous woollen material.

Dates and facts

1962	9.1.	Production of the VW 1500 version begins.
	20.11.	Heinrich Nordhoff officially opens the new VW centre in the USA at Englewood Cliffs. In the USA there are 15 distributors and 687 dealers operating.
	Dec.	3,330 Beetles are produced daily.

Above and below right:
The crest is removed from the bonnet lid. The moulding is longer as a result.

The 'folding' roof is still available on the Export Saloon until August 1963.

Headlining is made of plastic; formerly cloth.

Export model: Air outlets with regulating lever in the heel-boards.

In December all engines are fitted with fresh air heating (heat exchangers) identifiable by the two thick air hoses coming from the fan housing.

1962 The most important modifications

Year	Chassis No.	No.	Modification
Engine/clutch/heating			
23.2.62	4 519 277	6 502 426	Crankcase vent: connecting pipe on the underside of the oil-bath air filter. Formerly on the air intake.
28.5.62	4 745 703	6 754 500	Engine oil: initial fill quantity 2.5l SAE10 mixed with 1 per cent Lubrizol. Formerly: 1.75l.
3.5.62	4 683 160	6 179 146	Clutch: all pressure springs coloured brown. Formerly 3 yellow and 3 grey-blue pressure springs.
30.7.62	4 846 836	6 916 251	Oil cooler: with air filter. Induction manifold and pre-heating pipe: diameter of pipe at connecting flange to cylinder head 27 mm. Formerly 25 mm. Cooling fan housing/fan: shape altered, resulting in greater efficiency. Cylinder head: induction port 27 mm diameter. Formerly 25 mm.
2.8.62	4 874 267	3 942 539	Crankcase vent oil vapour is drawn into the oil-bath air filter. Formerly released to atmosphere.
21.9.62	4 988 623	7 076 057	Piston and piston rings: depth of two upper piston ring grooves reduced by 0.6 mm. New piston rings with chamfer on the inner rim.
5.10.62	5 020 751	7 115 342	Engine oil initial fill-up: SAE10W. Formerly SAE20.
15.12.62	5 199 980	7 336 420	Fresh air heating: air
15.12.62	5 199 981	3 949 223	heated in heat exchangers. Formerly by the cylinder fins.
15.12.62	5 199 980	–	Heating: heating ducts between silencer and bodywork isolated with plastic tubing.
Fuel system			
15.1.62	4 432 260	6 424 690	Fuel pump: pump operating lever as pressed part. Pressure spring lengthened. Formerly two-part casting.
9.4.62	4 636 869	6 660 578	Fuel line between pump and carburettor: pipe with flexible end pieces. Formerly rubber tubing with braided covering.

Year	Chassis No.	Assembly No.	Modification
Brakes/wheels/tyres			
5.4.62	4630938 (111/112) (115/116)	–	Brake system: hydraulic. Formerly mechanical.
18.9.62	4978442	–	Brake fluid reservoir: screw top. Formerly stopper.
Bodywork			
16.1.62	4420885	–	Doors: bottom and side clip attachment holes for door panelling with rubber inserts. Oiled paper on inside panels of doors stuck down. Rubber seal on window glass and window lifter rail lengthened to improve water drainage. Additional slide strip for window regulator rubber seal.
28.4.62	4671926	–	Door hinges: secured with three bolts each. Formerly four bolts.
28.4.62	4672922	–	Window regulator: spring loaded in the guide rail.
16.5.62	4723425	–	Rear heating duct supporting cage in form of wire-netting tube with 2 asbestos rings. Formerly plastic.
30.7.62	4846836	–	Handle for sliding roof: flatter and hinged. Window guides: plastic. Formerly: fabric. Headlining now plastic. Formerly woollen material.
30.7.62	4763158 (141-144)	–	VW badge: lettering 'VOLKSWAGEN'.
1.8.62	(141,143)	–	Paintwork: Polar Blue, Earth Brown, Manila Yellow, Emerald Green. Continued lines: Black, Pearl White, Ruby, Anthracite, Sea Blue, Pacific. Discontinued: Paprika Red, Lavender, Pampas Green, Sierra Biege.
1.10.62	5010448 (113–118)	–	Bonnet lid: VW emblem newly incorporated. Formerly badge with crest. Moulding extended.
13.12.62	5188470	–	Footwell heating, rear: outlets with regulating levers.
Electrics			
15.12.62	5199980	7336420	Spark plug terminals now with plastic safety caps.

1963

The 'folding' roof is discontinued on the Export model (available on Standard model until 1.8.67); the roof panel is made smaller to accommodate a crank-operated steel sunroof as an optional extra. The casing of the new number plate light has a broad, slightly curved form, which gives a new styling to the contours of the rear of the vehicle. Bulb socket and lens are taken from the number plate light of the Type 3 Saloon (VW 1500). The modified curve of the engine lid is adapted to the new number plate light.

In November of this year newly shaped, broader indicator lights are fitted: as a result, installation on the front wings is changed.

The steering wheel with semi-circular horn ring is replaced by a steering wheel with thumb buttons for the horn.

The embossed VW emblem in the chrome-finished hub-caps is no longer highlighted in black.

VW achieves a turnover of 6.84 Billion marks. This puts it at the head of all German industrial concerns. VW has a 42.4 per cent share of German car production. At home VW manufactures 1,029,591 cars and abroad 77,511 cars. With a total of 685,769 cars exported VW is the largest automobile exporter in the world. At the primary factory at Wolfsburg a fully automatic line for the assembly of Beetle bodywork starts operation. Daily production by the middle of the year stands at 5,229 units.

Dates and facts

1963	August	New model: VW 1500S Saloon Variant, Coupé). 54 bhp, 2 Solex down-draught carburettors, 880 kg, price 6400 DM. This year, more than one out of every two cars exported from the Federal Republic is a Volkswagen.
	Sept.	At the Australian VW assembly plant at Clayton/Victoria the assembly begins of the VW 1500 and Variant in September.

Wider number plate light gives the vehicle's rear end a new look. The curvature of the engine lid is adapted to suit the contours of the new number plate light.

88

As an extra, the Export Saloon can be fitted with a steel sliding sun roof with a retractable crank handle.

The VW emblem in the hub caps is no longer highlighted in black.

Larger flashing indicator lights on the front wings.

Steering wheel with thumb button horn; semi-circular ring is discontinued.

1963 The most important modifications

Year	Chassis No.		Assembly No.	Modification
Engine/clutch/heating				
1.10.63	5815778		8046097	Crankcase vent: new sludge draining pipe with rubber vent.
19.12.63	6009513 (Export)		8250020	Rocker mechanism: valve angle increased. Rocker shaft repositioned. Cylinder head, rockers and push rods modified.
Front axle/steering				
5.8.63	5677119	(113/114) (117/118) (141/152)	–	Steering wheel: twin thumb buttons for horn. Formerly horn ring.
10.9.63	5765471		–	Shock absorbers: single tube absorbers with plastic protective sleeves. Piston rods pull in a downward direction.
Brakes/wheels/tyres				
5.8.63	5677119	(113/114) (117/118)	–	Hub caps: VW emblem no longer highlighted in colour.
5.8.63	5677119		–	Tyres 5.60-15: rear tyre pressure 1.7 bar. Formerly: 1.6 bar.
Chassis				
28.10.63	5875847		–	Upper part of chassis: rear cut-out section for gear change shaft coupling enlarged.
Bodywork				
1.2.63		(111-112) (115-116)	–	Paintwork: Gulf Blue. Continued lines: Jupiter Grey, Reed Green.
1.4.63	5419871		–	Seal around bumper bracket: plastic. Formerly rubber.
3.4.63	5440221		–	Front seat backrest adjustment: contact surfaces of adjusting cam enlarged.
5.8.63	5677119	(111/112) (115/116)	–	Control knobs and steering wheel: silver beige colour. Formerly black. Roof panelling: synthetic. Formerly, fabric.

Year	Chassis No.		Assembly No.	Modification
				Seats: synthetic covering. Formerly fabric.
5.8.63	5677119	(111-118) (151-152)	–	Door seals now foam material. Interior trim panels on doors. Formerly: leather and oiled paper on the inner skin.
5.8.63	5677119	(117/118)	–	Volkswagen 1200 Export: crank-operated steel sun roof. Formerly folding roof.
5.8.63	5677119 5718489	(113/114) (117/118) (151/152)	– – –	Engine lid: shape of curve altered; securing holes for number plate light moved.
5.8.63	5718489	(141-144)	–	Door lock: internal operating mechanism altered.
5.8.63	5677119	(111/112) (115/116)	–	Paintwork: Sea Blue, Anthracite, Pearl White, Ruby. Discontinued: Reed Green, Jupiter Grey, Gulf Blue.
15.8.63	5699145		–	Door: Door stay has 90 degree bend at rubber buffer. Formerly: restraining peg.
31.10.63	5888185		–	Wing and side panels at the front: new: drillings altered by repositioning of indicator lights.

Electrics

Year	Chassis No.		Assembly No.	Modification
19.10.63	5851619	(141-144)	–	Windscreen washer: washer reservoir built-in.
31.10.63	5888185		–	Flashing indicator lights at front: shape altered.

1964

The most striking modification takes place in the bodywork: by incorporating slimmer pillars and a gently curved windscreen which extends 28 mm further into the roof, the angles of vision have been markedly improved. The rear window is around 20 mm higher and 10 mm wider; door windows and quarter light are enlarged; smaller cross-sections of the door window frames make this possible. The pillar between door window and quarter light is no longer vertical, but slants. In concept with enlargement of the door window glasses the single arm window raiser is replaced by a cable operated window raiser. The locking handle of the quarter light no longer has a push button release. The latch is thus easy to operate when driving.

The T-handle on the engine lid is replaced by a push button handle made of high-grade chrome finished steel. The catch engages itself automatically when the lid is lowered.

The rear seat rest folds right down and can be secured by an adjustable strap.

The sun visors are a new shape and can be swivelled sideways also. The cooling air regulation of the 34 bhp engine has been moved to the discharge side of the fan. For this reason the control ring formerly attached to the fan housing is discontinued. The new cooling air control reduces the engine warming-up time.

The rotating heating control is now replaced by two swivel levers. The right lever (red knob) operates the heating. The left lever (white knob) controls the flaps of the rear footwell heating.

The new swivel levers enable the heating to be operated more quickly.

In line with the new enlarged windscreen the windscreen wiper mechanism is modified also. Spring cushioned wiper blades, lengthened by exactly 15 mm, give a broader sweep. On the Export model and the Cabrio the parking position of the wipers is switched to the left side.

The car jack, previously fitted with a single levering point, now has two, one for raising, one for lowering. The second point enables the vehicle to be lowered slowly. The Standard Beetle is now fitted with the fully synchromesh four-speed gearbox familiar on the Export model.

VW invests 154.4 million DM this year in the new assembly plant in Emden and 44.5 million DM for the expansion of the assembly plant at Port Elizabeth (South Africa) begun in March.

A total of 68 specially designed ships with 550,000 registered tonnage transport 470,000 Volkswagens to export countries, mainly to America. The chartering fees for the ships total 150 million marks per year.

Around 89,000 former VW savers stake their claims in March, of which 8,200 are accepted. After the settlement of 18.10.1961 each saver receives according to the original sum invested up to 600 DM discount on a VW 1200 or up to 100 DM in cash. Up to now 18,000 Beetles are delivered to the savers and 41,000 compensation payments are given out.

Dates and facts

1964   23.10.   Daimler Benz and Volkswagen announce their intention to work together. The co-operation extends at first to the Auto Union GmbH Ingolstadt, which they want to run together. The 80 million DM ordinary share capital of Auto Union, in the possession of DB, is raised by a further 80 million DM; VW takes over a total of 50.4 per cent of the Auto Union ordinary share capital.

        1.12.   Production begins in the new Volkswagen factory in Emden. For the first time wages and salaries in the VW joint stock company exceed 1 Billion DM.

The rear window is 20 mm higher and 10 mm wider.

Right: larger window surfaces all round.

Slimmer door window frames allow the door windows to be extended upwards and rearwards. The pillar between quarter light and door window slants backwards.

The gently curved windscreen extends a further 28 mm into the roof. The wipers come to rest on the left.

The locking catch of the quarter light no longer has a push-button release.

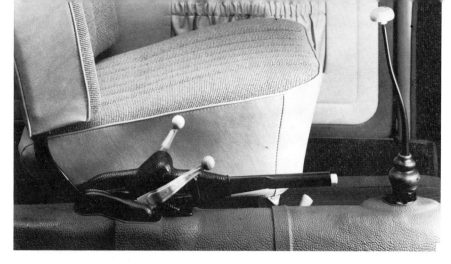

In place of the rotating heating operating lever on the central tunnel are (left-hand lever) grey knob for rear footwell heating and (right-hand lever) red knob for the heat control.

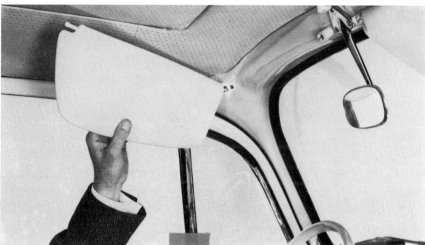

Newly shaped sun visor swivels to the side.

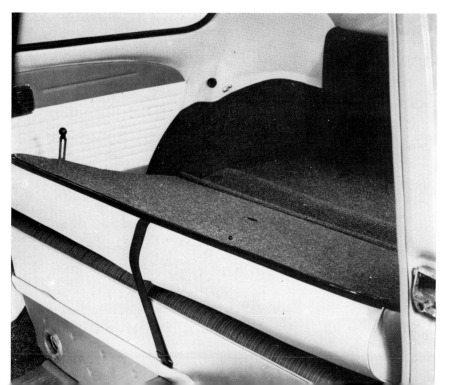

The rear seatrest folds right down and is held down by a strap.

T-handle replaced now by push button catch made of high grade chrome-finished steel.

Cutaway picture of the redesigned Model 65 Beetle.

Cabrio: Courtesy light attached to top of windscreen frame.

1964

The most important modifications

Year	Chassis No.	Assembly No.	Modification
Engine/clutch/heating			
21.3.64	6223768 (Export)	8487010	Oil filter cover plate sealed with cap nuts and copper washers. Formerly hexagon nuts and spring washers. Gasket material changed.
7.10.64	115162922	HA7256130	Release bearing: now with plastic ring. Formerly with graphite ring.
8.10.64	115162787	8963731	Clutch disc 180 and 200 mm diameter. Splines in the hub phosphate-treated. Splines of input drive shaft treated with molybdenum disulphide.
6.11.64	115262699	–	Silencer optionally enamelled in dark blue.
7.12.64	115336420 (1200A)	–	Oil-bath air filter: now with crankcase ventilation.
Rear axle/gears			
3.8.64	115000001	7022722	Rear wheel bearing: housing: oil deflector in front of seal. Rear wheel bearing: bearing housing and brake back plate with drainage hole. Formerly oil trap.
30.10.64	115247529 (1200A)	7356688	Volkswagen 1200A: full synchromesh gears. Formerly partial synchromesh gears.
Brakes/wheels/tyres			
3.8.64	115000001	–	Brake back plate and brake shoes: additional contact surfaces on brake back plate (three-point support). Slots for adjusters and brake cylinder pistons increased in diameter. Angled mounting of the brake shoes. Box shaped bearing bracket. Rear brake drum: drilling in oil trap for fastening discontinued.
Chassis			
3.8.64	115000001	–	Heater operation: guide sleeve for heater flap cable discontinued. Heater operating levers mounted alongside bearing bracket for handbrake lever. Right lever (red knob) operates overall heating. Left lever (white knob) activates rear footwell outlets.

Year	Chassis No.	Assembly No.	Modification
			Both ducts for heater cables moved to right-hand side of chassis tunnel. Additional two ducts for activating rear heating outlets moved to left-hand side: these exist at each side of the chassis tunnel, behind the heelboards. Chassis number on chassis tunnel: bordered at each end by an inlaid star symbol.
24.10.64	115224816	–	Adjusting nut for clutch cable: now wing nut. Formerly hexagon nut.

Bodywork

Year	Chassis No.	Assembly No.	Modification
5.2.64	6130478 (151/152)	–	Moulding for running board: chromed steel. Formerly aluminium.
1.7.64	6483093	–	Wax preservative: now fully coated with preservative. Formerly part treated.
3.8.64	115000001	–	Windows: enlarged window areas.
3.8.64	115000001	–	Engine cover with latch: push button latch. Formerly: lock with handle and lock plate. Stops on the lid hinges 12 mm high. Formerly 7 mm.
3.8.64	115000001	–	Interior furnishings: front seat backrests thinner and more compliant. Outer backrest tube fitted with springs. Backrest can be tipped forward and held with a strap to increase luggage space. Sun visors enlarged and shape altered. Supported by swivels on the windscreen surround. Formerly, on rear view mirror.
3.8.64	115000001	8796623	Heater operation: by lever. Formerly by turning handle.
3.8.64	115000001	–	Window raiser: cable operated window raiser. Formerly single-arm window raiser.
3.8.64	115000001	–	Car jack with two levering joints, one for raising, one for lowering. Formerly one levering joint.
3.8.64	115000001(1200A)	–	Paintwork: fontana grey. Continued lines: Ruby, Sea Blue, Pearl White. Discontinued: Anthracite.

Year	Chassis No.	Assembly No.	Modification
	(Export)	–	Paintwork: Fontana Grey. Continued lines: Black, Ruby, Sea Blue, Pearl White, Panama Beige, Java Green, Bahama Blue. Discontinued: Anthracite.
1.10.64	115161388	–	External mirror: adhesive backing for rear of mirror glass.

Electrics

Year	Chassis No.	Assembly No.	Modification
3.8.64	115000001	–	Windscreen wipers: sprung wiper blades parking on left. Formerly on right.
3.8.64	115000001	8788071	Distributor: cam now asymmetrical. Cam of third cylinder retarded 2°.
1.12.64	115331161	9129761	Spark plugs: Champion L87V. Continued types: Bosch W175 T1, Beru 175/14 and Champion L85.

General modifications

Year	Chassis No.	Assembly No.	Modification
3.8.64	115000001	–	Chassis No: nine digits. Formerly seven digits.
30.10.64	115247429 (1200A)	7356688	Volkswagen 1200A: full synchromesh gears.

1965

New to the series is the VW 1300, driven by a 1.3-litre 40 bhp engine. The crankshaft from the 1.5-litre (Type 3) is transferred to the new 1300 engine. As a result the stroke is raised from 64 to 69 millimetres.

The hallmark of the new year's model is the perforated steel disc wheels. The apertures in the wheel rim not only enhance the vehicle's looks, but also reduce the weight of the unsprung parts.

All Beetle models are fitted with new brake drums, whose hubs have star shaped ribs for reinforcement.

To distinguish the 40 bhp engine Volkswagen from its smaller brother, the engine lid now has a '1300' badge fixed to the left-hand side

A new front axle is fitted, construction being a cross between the former Beetle axle and the front axle of the VW 1500. On the new axle the steering knuckle and control arms are linked via maintenance-free ball joints. The modified torsion bars together with revised shock absorbers and new hollow rubber buffers all serve to give a much more comfortable suspension. While the lubrication nipples on the steering knuckles are discontinued, the axle tubes (4 lubrication nipples) must still be lubricated every 10,000 km.

More new features on the 1300 Saloon and the four-seater Cabrio include: a locking mechanism on the front seat rests to prevent their folding forward unintentionally; an additional demister in the middle of the dashboard to facilitate quicker defrosting of the windscreen; a semi-circular horn ring on the steering wheel; and the headlight flasher is operated by the indicator stalk.

Volkswagen builds an assembly line for the VW 1200 on the Auto Union site in Ingolstadt.

This further assembly line raises daily VW production to 6,000 vehicles, 4,550 of these being Beetles. With total purchases of over 4 billion Marks the concern ranks as the largest private contractor in the Federal Republic of Germany.

Dates and facts

1964	5.1.	Volkswagen acquires Auto Union GmbH from Daimler-Benz.
	9.3.	The VW 147 small delivery van is put on show, developed in collaboration with the German Post Office and designed and assembled at the Westphalia works in Wiedenbrück. The public christen it 'Fridolin'. The first delivery of the vehicle to the German Post Office is made simultaneously.
	12.7.	Transport and haulage operations are to be carried out by the newly founded subsidiary, the 'Wolfsburger Transportgesellschaft mbH'.
	6.8.	New Type 3 model: VW 1600TL ('Fastback').
	15.9.	10 million Volkswagens since the end of the war!
	Dec.	In the research and development centre of the Wolfsburg works the most modern wind tunnel in Europe begins operation.

New 1.3-litre engine with 40 bhp. The diaphragm valve, until now installed between fuel pipe and fuel pump, is now to be found in the fuel pump.

Flattened wheel hub caps from the VW 1500 (Type 3); apertures in the wheel rims.

New to the series: VW 1300 with 1.3-litre/40 bhp engine. '1300' badge on the engine.

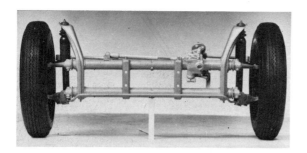

The redesigned front axle has 10-leaf torsion bars. Maintenance-free balljoints connect the steering knuckles to the torsion arms. The 4 lubrication nipples in the axle tubes need lubrication only every 10,000 km.

VW 1300 and Cabrio: additional demister vent in the middle of the dashboard. Dip switch and headlamp flasher on the indicator lever. Semi-circular horn ring, on which the thumb bars remain in a slightly altered form.

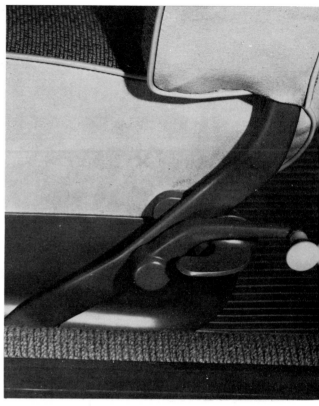

The backrests of the front seats have a locking mechanism to prevent their falling forwards unintentionally.

Door safety lock, in which the safety plate prevents the door springing open during violent flexing of the body.

Door and side panel trims have horizontal bright strips.

VW 1200A: 1.2-litre/34 bhp engine. New front axle, slotted steel disc wheels. Seat and back rest adjustment as in VW 1300. Motif on the engine cover 1200.

Cabrio: apertures in the wheels rims seen here with extra wheel trims. Flat hub caps.

Foot-operated dip switch remains only on the 1200 Saloon.

1965

The most important modifications

Year	Chassis No.	Assembly No.	Modification
Engine/clutch/heating			
1.3.65	115579323	9282492	Clutch lining (180 mm diam.) radial grooves on flywheel side.
6.4.65	115685587	HA7889618	Clutch lever now straight, with wing nut for adjusting the clutch cable. Formerly curved, with ball nut for adjustment.
31.5.65	115855772	9623350	Heat exchanger: heater flap spindle galvanised.
2.8.65	116000001 (1200A)	D0000001	Crankcase: separate bushes for camshaft. Formerly, running in the case. Cylinders – 1200A and 122: 18 cooling fins. Formerly 12. Cylinders – 1500, 124A and 126A: 19 cooling fins. Formerly 14.
15.12.65	116407142	HA8729521	Clutch release bearing: synthetic ring treated with molybdenum disulphide.
Fuel system			
24.6.65	115946462	–	Sealing for tank cap: rubber. Formerly cork.
Front axle/steering			
2.8.65	116000001	–	Front axle unit: distance between axle tubes 150 mm. Formerly 120 mm. Torsion bars: 10-leaf. Formerly 8-leaf. Torsion arm link: Inner bush in metal. Formerly synthetic bush. Steering stub axle: connected to the torsion arms by maintenance-free balljoints. Upper joint has eccentric bush with which the camber can be precisely adjusted. Steering 1200A: worm and roller steering. Formerly worm and sector steering.
15.10.65	116232227	–	Wheel bearing adjustment: slot of clamp nut 2.5 + 0.5 mm. Formerly 2.0 – 0.5 mm.
Chassis			
29.12.65	116460614	–	Progressive accelerator pedal: now with a hinged curved plate, running on roller attached to the cable lever. Throttle cable: 2627 mm long (left-hand drive). Formerly 2650 mm. 2635 mm

Year	Chassis No.	Assembly No.	Modification
			long (right-hand drive). Formerly 2615 mm.

Bodywork

Year	Chassis No.	Assembly No.	Modification
18.1.65	115460398	–	Moulding for door windows: plastic guide stops on the decorative trim discontinued.
31.3.65	115623180	–	Door trim panel: PVC layer on the reverse.
15.6.65	115928504 (1200A)	–	Support for bonnet: spring loaded. Formerly slotted into place, and disengaged manually.

Electrics

Year	Chassis No.	Assembly No.	Modification
5.3.65	115594027	9285001	Ignition leads: with copper cores, resistors for spark plug connectors (1 Kilo-ohm) and suppressed distributor. Formerly resistor ignition leads.
9.3.65	115574730	9273966	Distributor: suppressed.

General modifications

Year	Chassis No.	Assembly No.	Modification
18.2.65	115553822 115558010 (1200A)	9247364 3991433	Engine identification: all engines are given a letter according to the horsepower rating. A VW symbol is stamped before the letter.

Engine rating	Letter
30 hp	A
34 hp	D
40 hp	F

1966

The most striking modification to the bodywork occurs on the engine cover. The lower section is now shorter, the seating for the registration plate now being more vertical in accordance with the stipulations of the various export countries. As a consequence of this modification the engine compartment is enlarged, so allowing easier engine removal.

The new chrome trim is narrower, giving a more elegant look and a more discreet emphasis to the exterior contours.

The new 1.5-litre engine achieves its 44 bhp at 4000 revs, the highest torque of 102 nm occurring now at 2000 rpm. Top speed with the new engine is 125 km/h, the Ghia models reaching 132 km/h. Besides the increased capacity, the chief change is the intake air pre-heating: the air is drawn from the cooling air of both cylinder heads through two pipes and mixed with the intake air.

All Beetle models are fitted with an equalizer spring on the rear axle. The spring assists the action of the rear torsion bars. At the same time the cars have a wider rear track, now 1350 mm.

In keeping with the higher engine performance the VW 1500 is fitted with disc brakes at the front.

An often heard customer request is met with the new key system. The ignition/starter lock can now be operated with the same key that locks the doors.

The doors can be locked by a button in the lower rear corner of the window frame.

The driver's door has an arm rest that also serves as a handle for shutting the door.

The backrest locking mechanism is now located in the seat backs.

Window winders, light switches and the switch for the windscreen wipers have been fitted with knobs of soft plastic. They are black, to prevent reflections in the windscreen.

All Beetle models are fitted with an 'early cut-in' dynamo, the regulator for which is mounted inside the car on the left-hand side under the rear seat. The fuse box now has 10 instead of 8 fuses. One of the additional fuses is for the windscreen wiper motor, a spare for the other accessories added subsequently.

In place of the VW 1200, the VW 1300A is introduced, which can be fitted optionally with a 34 or a 40 bhp engine.

In 1966 VW's share capital is increased from 600 to 750 million DM. VW as a whole has produced over 12 million vehicles; 2 million alone have been exported to the USA.

The service network is extended in the Federal Republic to 2,287 garages and in the rest of Europe to 2,972.

1966 June Volkswagen and Daimler Benz AG jointly found the German Automobile Association (Deutsche Automobil-gesellschaft mbH), based in Hanover. Its task, amongst others, is the intensification of research and development.

18.10. 'Volkswagen Leasing GmbH', Wolfsburg is founded.

New to the series: the VW 1500 Beetle Saloon with 44 bhp engine.

Dates and facts

25.11. The 12 millionth VW comes off the production line. This includes 9 million Beetles, 1.2 million 1500s and 1600s and 1.8 million Transporters.

Nov. The Volkswagen concern acquires 19.2 per cent of the capital of the Brazilian Auto-Union firm Vemag (the third largest Brazilian vehicle producer).

1.5-litre engine with 44 bhp. The pre-heating of the intake air takes place via two pipes. A weighted regulator-flap in each intake duct controls the intake of the pre-heated air.

Narrower chrome trim marks the model year.

Motif on the engine hood is 'VW 1500'. The engine hood is shorter in the lower section, the surface for the number plate more vertical. The central rib is dropped, the number plate light is adapted to the new shape.

All switches have flat-head knobs in soft plastic. They are black to prevent reflections. The pull-knob for the ashtray is dropped. The regulator for the dynamo is located on the left-hand side under the rear seat.

The backrest catch is fitted into the seat back.

The door can be locked by a button in the rear corner of the window frame. The arm rest on the driver's door can be used also to shut the door.

Equalizing spring at the rear for all Beetle models.

Striker plate lock for increased security against door springing open.

Newly designed door handle. The ignition lock can be operated with the door key.

VW 1500: disc brakes on the front wheels. The wheels on this model are now secure with only 4 wheel bolts.

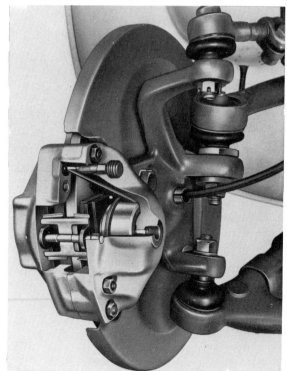

1966   The most important modifications

Year	Chassis No.	Assembly No.	Modification
Engine/clutch/heating			
3.1.66	116 471 044	FO 437 269	Sump plate: new tapping for thread of oil drain plug, with annular ring for seating. Formerly: thread plate welded in, no annular ring.
3.1.66	116 463 104 116 463 105	DO 050 315 FO 442 243	Heating pipe in left-hand heat exchanger now one piece. Formerly welded from two pieces.
7.1.66	116 478 507	FO 451 421	Con rod studs with nuts. Formerly bearing cap secured with hexagon screws.
10.2.66	116 561 017	FO 541 013	Gudgeon pin bush: steel with leaded bronze coat. Formerly brass.
3.5.66	116 807 190	DO 079 454	Carburettor pre-heating: warm air taken from the heat exchangers. Formerly extracted from underside of cylinder head.
23.6.66	116 975 949	FO 904 848	Push rod: lengthened by 0.8 mm to 9 mm. Formerly 8.14 mm.
1.8.66	117 000 002 (113/114)	HO 204 001	Engine: 44 bhp engine (1.5-litre)
15.8.66	117 054 916	HO 225 117	Oil pressure relief valve: piston with annular groove. Formerly without groove.
29.9.66	117 197 986 117 198 502	FO 991 728 HO 398 526	Crankcase studs M12 x 1.5 at bearing 2: sealing rings between crankcase halves. Formerly self-sealing nuts.
25.11.66	117 359 672	HO 507 977	Oil pipe: seamless pipe. Formerly welded pipe.
7.12.66	117 374 455	HO 530 628	Big-end bearing cap: radius at the bearing surface of the stud 2.5 mm. Formerly 4 mm radius.
3.1.66	116 463 104 (1200 A)	DO 050 315	Carburettors 28 and 30 PICT-1: carburettor body – upper part with bracket for throttle return.
1.4.66	116 723 046 116 723 047	DO 071 815 FO 684 881	Fuel pump: split plastic guide for diaphragm pushrod. Formerly rubber sleeve. Fuel pumps – upper part: gasket between cover and diaphragm.

Year	Chassis No.	Assembly No.	Modification
Front axle/steering			
1.8.66	117 000 003 (1500)	–	Front axle: now with disc brake. Formerly drum brake. Steering stub axle altered.
1.8.66	117 000 002 (111/112) (115/116)	–	Steering wheel: two-spoke wheel with deep set hub. Formerly three-spoke.
2.9.66	117 112 756	8590 035	Steering track-rod: track-rod outer end secured with damping sleeve and inner end with control nut. Intermediate rod and locking plate discontinued. Formerly: adjustable at right-hand track rod end and in the centre.
Rear axle/gears			
1.8.66	117 000 001	–	Rear suspension: with equalizer spring (except Type 147 and 1200 with Saxomat).
Brakes/wheels/tyres			
1.8.66	117 000 001	–	Brake back plate at rear: with two adjustment and two inspection holes.
1.8.66	117 000 003 (1500)	–	Front wheels: disc brakes: formerly drum brakes.
1.8.66	117 000 003 (1500)	–	Hubs for disc brakes: 4 wheel bolts M14 x 1.5, tightening torque 13 mkg, hole PCD 130 mm. Formerly: Five M12 x 1.5, torque 10 mkg, hole PCD 250 mm. Hub caps: shape changed. Wheel trims: adapted to the modified hubs.
17.11.66	117 349 409 (1500)	–	Brake fluid reservoir for single circuit brake system: installed 17 mm higher.
27.12.66	117 398 501	–	Hub caps: shape changed.
Chassis			
3.5.66	116 851 572	–	Pedals: brake and clutch pedal made from sheet steel. Formerly cast iron.
1.8.66	117 000 001	–	Chassis tunnel: water drainage hole with rubber valve in front of chassis fork.
Bodywork			
2.5.66	116 809 564	–	Door handle: new design; casing of Nirosta-steel.

Year	Chassis No.	Assembly No.	Modification
1.8.66	117 000 001	–	Door lock: locking plate secured with 4 screws. Formerly 3 screws
1.8.66	117 000 003	–	Exterior moulding: narrower profile, secured with plastic clips (except for moulding on door thresholds). Install-ation holes for clips smaller.
1.8.66	117 000 001	–	Engine compartment: sealing plate inside shortened. Engine cover plates narrower. Broader seal on the engine cover. New: Sound-proofing strength-ened around lower part of the rear window. Front sound-proofing 3 layers of material stuck together.
1.8.66	117 000 001	–	Door lock: single-key system.
1.8.66	117 000 001	–	Interior fittings: control knobs of flexi-ble plastic: ashtray with recess for gripping. Recessed remote handles for door locks. Door and side trim panel-ling altered.
1.8.66	117 000 001	–	Rear quarters: along with the reinfor-cements to the wheel arch, change of shape to accommodate the equalizer spring.
1.8.66	117 000 001	–	Engine cover: shape changed. Engine rear sealing plate: adapted to accom-modate cover. Interior tinware nar-rower, and moulding modified to ac-commodate broader rubber seal.
1.12.66	117 425 908	–	Front seat backrest lock: operated by knob in upper part of backrest. Formerly in seat base.

Electrics

Year	Chassis No.	Assembly No.	Modification
1.8.66	117 000 002 (111/112) (115/116)	–	Steering wheel: indicator switch and horn button changed (two-spoke steer-ing wheel).
1.8.66	117 000 001	–	Starter: smaller pinion diameter (fly-wheel and transmission casing al-tered).
1.8.66	117 000 001	–	Steering ignition lock: tongue lock. Lock barrel can be pushed in ("single key system"). Formerly: pin lock (ig-nition key separate). New: Model 14 – steering-starter switch. Formerly: ig-nition lock with ignition/starter switch.
1.8.66	117 000 001	Certain export countries only	Headlights: now fitted vertically (sealed – beam headlights). Side light

113

Year	Chassis No.	Assembly No.	Modification
			(parking light) accommodated in front indicator light. Wing changed.
1.8.66	117 000 001	–	Fuse box: 10 fuse clips.
1.8.66	117 000 001 117 000 002 117 000 003	DO 095 050 FO 940 717	Distributor: modified. Ignition coil: with three connections to terminal 15 (except Type 147). Formerly two connections.
1.8.66	117 000 001 (111/118) (151/152)	–	Stop lights: bulb sockets for stop light modified.
1.8.66	117 000 001	–	Windscreen wiper motor: Model 14: two wipe speeds (same modification on Model 11 and 15 with optional extra 12v). Formerly no regulation. Switch for windscreen wiper motor: rotary switch. Formerly pull switch.
1.8.66	117 000 001	–	Reverse light (M47): two reversing lights mounted on rear bumpers.
22.8.66	117 050 500	–	Fuel gauge: Bowden cable secured with a clip.
3.10.66	117 199 633	FO 993 239	Ignition coil, 6 volts: with two spade terminals at terminal 15. Formerly one connector.
5.10.66	117 207 566	FO 950 336	Ignition coil, 12 volt: with two spade connectors at terminal 15. Formerly one connector.
8.12.66	117 383 344	HO 533 523	Spark plugs: heat value 145 (only on engines with battery ignition, Type 122 and 126A). Formerly 175.

1967

The bumpers are significantly strengthened and are raised. Thus both engine cover and bonnet must be shortened, and the valances must be raised.

The engine lid, with new lock and handle, is fitted with an additional catch hook, which has a push button released.

The front wings are redesigned to accommodate vertically-set headlights. The decorative grilles in the front wings of the Export Saloon are discontinued.

The bonnet now has louvres to let in fresh air. The fresh air is taken via a fresh air box and two tubes to the outlets by the windscreen.

The modified door latches are operated by a trigger incorporated into the door handle, and are so designed to make it impossible to lock oneself out by mistake. The tank filler neck is accessible from outside. The enlarged outside mirror can swivel round up to the door window if knocked.

All Beetle models are fitted with safety steering. So that three point seat belts can be fitted, the appropriate securing points are added. On Beetle 1300/1500 models the brake system is divided into two brake circuits. The tandem brake master cylinder reservoir is bolted to the left-hand side panel in the luggage compartment. In the speedometer dial all important warning lights and a petrol gauge are incorporated. On impact the interior mirror releases itself from its anchorage.

In conjunction with the semi-automatic gearbox, the 1500 Beetle is fitted with a completely new, technically sophisticated, double-jointed rear axle.

VW 1300 and 1500 are equipped with 12V electrics. In conjunction with this, all voltage-related parts of the electrics are modified.

The new rear light has a larger lens surface for greater safety. The newly fitted reversing lights are incorporated in the rear light casing. In conjunction with the newly designed steering ignition lock, the indicator switch has also been modified.

In August 1966 production of the 34 bhp VW. 1200 was halted (if requested, the VW 1300A was available with 34 bhp engine), and then, less than six months later (January 67) is put on the market again. It will remain in production until the end of the Beetle under the name *Sparkäfer* ('Economy Beetle'). The renewed production of the VW1200 is a response to the ever-more marked slacking of turnover. The 'Economy Beetle' costs 4,485 DM, the 40 bhp VW1300A 4,735 DM.

Dates and facts

1967	Aug.	The 'new Transporter' appears.
	Sep.	The NSU Ro80 comes out at the International Motor Show in Frankfurt. 115 bhp twin rotor Wankel engine; twin carburettors and spark plugs; engine weight 100 kg; 175 km/h top speed. Vehicle weight 1,210 kg; price 14,150 DM.
		VW Bus-Taxi from Wiedenbrück, Westphalia. It holds 5 passengers, with bullet proof partition, central seat, sliding doors on both sides.
	Nov.	VW production begins in the new Volkswagen factory in Puebla, Mexico with the 1200 model.

Reinforced and raised bumpers. As a result bonnet and engine cover shortened and valances raised. Shorter exhaust tailpipes to fit in with the changes to the rear bodywork.

Modified front wings with vertical headlights. The decorative grilles in the front wings are dropped (except on VW1200).

Rear light with larger lens surface. Reverse lights as optional extra.

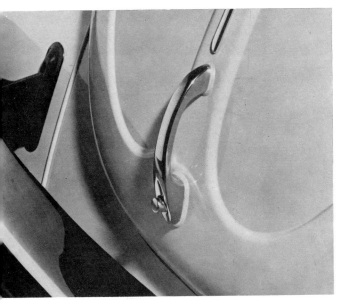

Newly designed handle for bonnet, with push button and additional catch hook.

Petrol tank filler neck in the right-hand front side panel, with flap.

VW 1300 and 1500:
Fresh air ventilation; air louvres in bonnet cover.

The distributor for the fresh air ventilation is located at the front in the centre of the instrument panel.

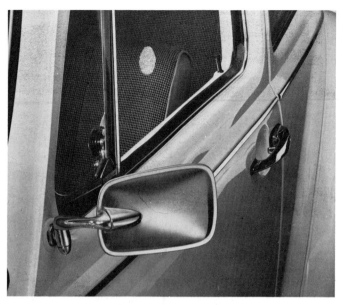

Enlarged exterior rear-view mirror. Operation of the catch for the quarter-light changed, deformable twist knob.

The door locks are operated by a trigger set into the door handle.

Optional extras include padding for the dashboard. All control knobs are flatter, broader and marked with symbols.

The combination instrument incorporates the petrol gauge and all the important warning lights. The steering ignition lock is encased in the steering column shroud. In the dashboard, three air outlets are provided.

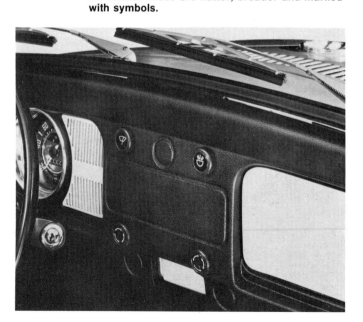

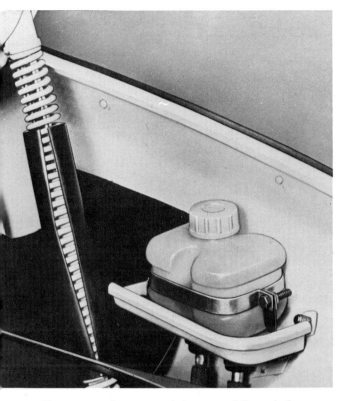

The new washer reservoir is secured through the spare wheel by two wedges.

The interior rear view mirror is coated in plastic and has a safety-release incorporated if it is struck.

VW 1300 and 1500: dual-circuit brakes. The brake fluid reservoir is situated at the front in the luggage compartment on the left side.

Shorter, straight, gear lever is moved 78 mm to the rear. Hand brake lever therefore also shortened.

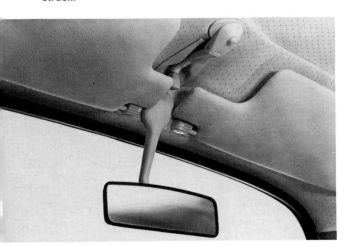

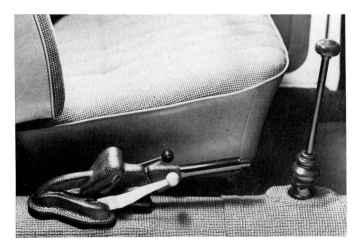

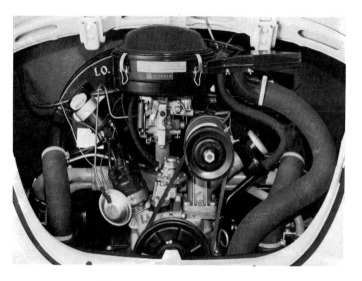

1.5-litre engine with new carburettor pre-heating and modified oil-bath air filter. VW 1300 and 1500 with 12 volt electrics.

Safety steering-column with crushable lattice section.

All Beetle models are fitted with the safety steering column, which in a crash collapses when the driver strikes the steering wheel.

Automatic Beetle with sophisticated, diagonal trailing arm rear axle.

1967   The most important modifications

Year	Chassis No.	Assembly No.	Modification
Engine/clutch/heating			
24.1.67	117493539 117489408 117488652	DO126605 F1064485 H0593766	Camshaft: stop collar on bearing 3 36.2 mm diam: Formerly: 34 mm diam.
26.6.67	117811587	HO823800	Crankshaft: double oil ways in 'X' arrangement. Oil pockets at entry apertures of passages. Formerly single oil-way.
26.6.67	117810605	F1162296	Clutch 180 mm diam. Torsion sprung clutch disc.
1.8.67	118000002 118000003 118000008 (M88)	FI237507 HO87200 DO234017	Exhaust: tail pipe 249 mm long. Formerly 276 mm long.
14.8.67	118054329	DO234159	Oil strainer: new funnel-shaped pick-up and spring loaded valve.
Fuel system			
1.8.67	118000001 (111-118)	–	Tank: Filler neck accessible via flap in right-hand front side panel. (Tank vent changed). Formerly underneath bonnet.
1.8.67	118000003 118000007 (M157)	HO874200 H5000001	Carburettor: 1.5- and 1.6-litre engines with 30 PICT – 2 carburettor with enlarged float chamber.
13.10.67	118233162	HO884591	Intake air pre-heating regulated by thermostat: new: Bowden cable 800 mm, conduit and spring of Type 2 incorporated. Formerly Bowden cable 650 mm long.
Front axle/steering			
11.4.67	117632001	–	Wheel bearing cap with opening for speedometer drive spindle: sealed with red metal cement. Formerly with sealing paint.
1.8.67	118000001	–	Steering: steering column with collapsible lattice section.
2.10.67	118164235	–	Wheel bearing cap with opening for speedometer spindle: sealed with special synthetic rubber cement. Formerly: with red metal cement.
Brakes/Wheels/Tyres			
1.8.67	118000002 (113/114) (115/116)	–	Brake drum at rear: brake shoe width 40 mm. Formerly 30 mm. Rear brake cylinder: 17.46 mm diam.

Year	Chassis No.	Assembly No.	Modification
1.8.67	118000002 (113/114) (117/118)	– –	Brake system: dual circuit brakes.
1.8.67	118000001	–	Brake fluid reservoir: moved into the front luggage compartment.
10.10.67	118227175	–	Pressed steel wheel: now with hump-rim.

Chassis

Year	Chassis No.	Assembly No.	Modification
20.4.67	117666265 (single circuit brakes)	–	Push rod for brake master cylinder: adjustable. Depression of clutch pedal: limited by stop behind pedal pad. (left-hand drive only).
1.8.67	118000001 (except 147)	–	Gear lever moved further back, shorter and straight.

Bodywork

Year	Chassis No.	Assembly No.	Modification
9.1.67	117470115	–	Bonnet handle: selectively of aluminium. Formerly Nirosta.
18.1.67	117496034	–	Door hinges: with oil reservoir.
1.8.67	118000001	–	Door latch: to be locked ony with key from the outside (home market only).
1.8.67	118000001 (115/116)	–	Sun roof: crank-operated steel sun roof. Formerly folding sun roof.
1.8.67	118000001	–	Safety belt: fastening points for fixing of lap, shoulder, or combined lap/shoulder belts.
1.8.67	118000001	–	Arm rest: horizontal.
1.8.67	118000001 (111-118)	–	Bumpers: reinforced U-profile, strengthened brackets, fixed higher, without bumper overriders (except 111/112, 115/116). Engine cover and bonnet: shortened. Valances adapted to modified covers. Front wings: vertically-mounted headlights, without decorative grille and aperture for horn (except 111/112, 115/116). Bonnet lock: additional catch hook, operated by push button. Bonnet lock cable: with soft plastic pull knob. In Cabriolet, control lever in lockable glove-compartment. Fresh air ventilation: central ventilation box inside front cowl panel; air enters through louvres in bonnet, regulation by rotary knobs.

Year	Chassis No.	Assembly No.	Modification
			Backrests on seats: locked at both sides, unlocked by cable release in left-hand side of backrest. Dashboard: available padded as luxury optional extra. Mirror: safety internal mirror with plastic surround. Outside mirror fastened on doors and larger. Front ashtray: *new:* tray when pulled out detaches itself automatically with pressure from above. Petrol tank filler neck: moved to right-hand side panel, accessible from outside.

Electrics

Year	Chassis No.	Assembly No.	Modification
1.8.67	118000001	–	Control knobs: flatter shape with pictures/symbols (soft plastic).
1.8.67	118000001	–	Windscreen wash reservoir: fitted inside spare wheel. Compressed air feed from spare wheel. Formerly fastened to cross-panel.
1.8.67	118000002 (113/114) (117/118)	–	Stop and rear lights: enlarged. Reverse lights fitted as optional extra.
1.8.67	118000001	–	Headlights: vertically mounted. (Wing modified).
1.8.67	118000001 (111-118)	–	Speedometer: thermo-electric fuel gauge built in.
1.8.67	118000002 (113/114) (117/118)	–	Horn: location changed, now under the bumper.
1.8.67	118000001	–	Steering column – mounted ignition switch: switch incorporated in column shroud.
	118000001	–	Interior light: bulb spring-loaded.
1.8.67	118000002 (113/114) (117/118) (141/144) (151/152)	–	Electrics: 12 volt. Formerly 6 volt. Battery: 12 V 36 Ah. Formerly 6 V 66 Ah.
1.9.57	118071448	HO879927	Distributor (automatic): with combined centrifugal and vacuum advance. Starter (automatic): pre-engaged starter 0.8 bhp (Bosch).

Year	Chassis No.	Assembly No.	Modification
27.10.67	118265979	–	Speedometer: driveshaft secured with circlip. Formerly with pin.
10.11.67	118328519 118327724	DO275833 FI261913	Oil pressure switch: fitted horizontally again. Formerly, from August 1967 (model year 1968) to November 1967, vertically-mounted.

General modifications

10.1.67	117483306	DO121136	VW-Saloon 1200 (M 86): production begins.
3.7.67	117839015	DO222312	Clutch, Saxomat (M 5): production halted.
1.9.67	118071448	HO879927	Volkswagen Type 1/1500 optionally fitted with semi-automatic gears.
10.10.67	118195200	H5077366	Volkswagen Type 1/1500: fitted with emission control and semi-automatic gears.

1968

The flap for the petrol tank filler is lockable. A cable pull to unlock it is located on the right underneath the dashboard.

The cable control to unlock the luggage compartment lid is located in the glove compartment.

The warm air outlets in the front footwell have been moved back to a position at the front edge of the seat rails, allowing more air to reach the windscreen. The fresh air outlets built into the dashboard are connected to the heating air ducts.

The seat backrest adjustment has four positions, so that in conjunction with the eight fore and aft seat positions, 32 possible seating positions are available. An indicator warning system is fitted as standard on all Beetle models. The speedo dial has been redesigned and can be read easily at a glance. The control lights are identified by symbols. The kilometer figures on the speedometer are vertically positioned.

Crankcase venting takes place in a closed circuit; the extraction hose is connected to the intake manifold of the oil-bath air filter. The oil-bath air filter of the VW 1500 engine now has only one intake pipe.

The 40 bhp VW 1300 can be fitted, optionally, with automatic gears and disc brakes (front). The internal safety mirror, designed to detach itself after a heavy jolt, is available as an anti-dazzle mirror (optional extra).

On 16 August 1968 Volkswagen introduces VW Diagnosis at all its 2,400 service garages at home.

The VW 1200 is fitted with a decorative grille in both wings. Up until now only the left mudguard had such a grille fitted.

Dates and facts

1968	5.2.	The 2 millionth Transporter rolls off the line in Hanover. Besides this VW built its 150,000th Automatic and its 100,000th vehicle with electronic fuel injection. Total daily production is 7,500 vehicles.
	19.3.	The 30,000th VW camper is manufactured in the Wiedenbrück, Westphalia, factory. The factory at Clayton (Victoria) of Volkswagen Australasia begins production of the VW 'Beach and Bush' car for the Australian market (forerunner of the VW 181).
	12.4.	After a brief illness Prof. Dr. Nordhoff dies at the age of 69.
	1.5.	Dr L.C. Kurt Lotz takes over as Chief Executive of the company.
	August	A new design appears; the VW 411, 2- and 4-door, with 68 bhp.
	29.11.	The 15 millionth Volkswagen since the end of the war rolls of the production line.
	9.12.	The newly founded Svenska Volkswagen AB in Sodertalje takes over the import of Volkswagens into Sweden, instead of Scania-Vabis. Volkswagen has a third share in the firm. VW Brazil brings the 4-door 'Brasilia' onto the market, as Saloon, to round off its range. On the South edge of the Lüneburg Heath not far from the village of Ehra an expensive test site is built, in which every imaginable driving condition can be tested. Up to the year's end the VW Foundation supports 2000 charities to the sum of over 930 Million DM.

Bonnet handle without push button. The bonnet is opened by a lever in the glove compartment. Flap for petrol filler can be locked.

Handle for unlocking petrol filler flap.
Underneath that is the lever for controlling warm
air outlets.

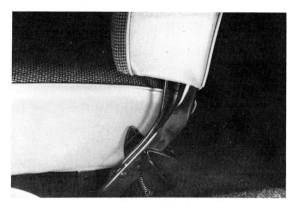

The warm air outlets in the front footwell have been moved to a position at the front edge of the seat rails.

The seat backrest adjustment works in a reverse sense to that used previously. When the lever is lifted the backrest moves into a more inclined position, when pressed down is more upright. The backrest can be reclined further than before.

The VW 1200 is fitted with a decorative grille in both front wings, rather than in the left one only.

1968

The most important modifications

Year	Chassis No.	Assembly No.	Modification
Engine/clutch/heating			
2.5.68	118799673	DO351591	Rocker cover: compressed cork
	118799674	FI403546	gasket. Formerly: flexolit.
	118799675	HO975667	
	118799676	H54325600	
	118799677	EO015534	
	118799678	LO020794	
29.5.68	118889936	H5359314	Clutch 200 mm diam: torsion-sprung
13.6.68	118960936	HO992155	clutch disc with single springs.
20.6.68	118971879	LO020951	Formerly: not torsion sprung.
13.6.68	118961796	HO992270	Oil pump housing (double oil pump):
	118963102	H5378841	size alteration of both gear sets and gaskets: gasket material copper/ asbestos. Formerly aluminium/ asbestos.
22.8.68	119058113	H5461147	Piston 83 mm diam. ovality changed.
19.9.68	119183797	H5501725	
5.11.68	119311485	HI044043	
Fuel system			
20.2.68	118582000	FI341000	Carburettor: 1.3-litre engine with 30 PICT-2 Carburettors with enlarged float chamber.
29.2.68	118613500	H5248586	Carburettor, Solex 30 PICT-2:
	118613135 (M9 + M157)	H5245666	carburettor housing upper section and
1.3.68	118613635	FI350553	lower section and sealing modified.
	118613636	HO945251	Idle air drilling in lower section.
	118613637 (M9)	HO945252	
18.4.68	118778781	H5302106	Fuel pipe on engine: zinc plated.
19.4.68	118781780	HO965312	Formerly copper plated.
22.4.68	118784587	FI390701	
	118784674	DO343622	
4.6.68	148932641 (141-144)	–	Petrol tank: filler hose linked by pipe.
	158932476	–	Connections fitted with additional
1.7.68	1181003668	–	clips. Formerly one-piece hose.
1.8.68	119000003	HI003256	Oil-bath air filter: weighted regulating
	119000009 (M9)	HI003257	flap in intake manifold. Air filters for
	119000007	H5414586	Types II and 15 1500 now have only
	119000010 (M9)	H5414587	One intake pipe with warm air regulating
	119000002	FI451086	flap and regulator flap for crankcase
	119000008 (M9)	FI462682	ventilation Type 1 1300 Automatic with

Year	Chassis No.	No.	Modification
			Bowden cable-controlled warm air flap in filter intake pipe. Wire cable now fastening on warm air flap lever by means of clip and eye. Wire cable 850 mm and casing 750 mm long. Formerly wire cable 800 mm and casing 700 mm long.

Front axle/steering

Year	Chassis No.	No.	Modification
6.5.68	118857240	375135	Front axle: track rod end spigot increased to 14 mm diam. Spigot thread changed to M12 x 1.5. Conical take-up bores for truck rod ends enlarged accordingly. Formerly: spigot diameter 12 mm. Spigot thread M 10 x 1.

Rear axle

Year	Chassis No.	No.	Modification
14.11.68	119340061	–	Equalizing spring: upper location of push-rod by silent block. Formerly with buffer stop.

Brakes

Year	Chassis No.	No.	Modification
3.1.68	148469038 (141-144)	–	Wheels: rim size $4^1/2$J x 15. Formerly 4J x 15.
1.8.68	119000001	–	Tyre valve: ring diameter 15.2 mm. Formerly 19.5 mm. Wheel: Valve hole diameter 11.5 mm. Formerly 16 mm.

Chassis

Year	Chassis No.	No.	Modification
27.3.68	118701827 (111-118)	–	Window lift: one-track design. Formerly two tracks. Window crankhandle with plastic covering.

Bodywork

Year	Chassis No.	No.	Modification
25.4.68	118739438	–	Sealing for crank-operated sun roof: new material 67 per cent Trevira, 33 per cent cotton-velvet. Formerly 100 per cent cotton-velvet.
21.6.68	118980404	–	Arm rest: safety arm rest without decorative trim (in USA from 1.8.67).
1.8.68	119000001	–	VW 1200: now with one decorative grille in each front wing.
1.8.68	119000001 (111-118) (141-144) (151-152)	– –	Heating/fresh air ventilation: heating pipe enlarged in cross-section. Rear outlet flaps additionally sealed

Year	Chassis No.	No.	Modification
			with silicon-rubber gaskets. Both fresh air outlets connected to the heating air ducts (except 1200 A). Front footwell outlets moved to position opposite seat rails. Flaps operated (formerly sliding) by wire cables. Front seats: The right-hand side of the seat frame is provided with a stop, and the corresponding guide rail fitted with a spring strip. Emergency seating, Model 14: seat wells installed in bench and backrest. Front seats – model 14: available with head rests as luxury optional extra. Flap for petrol tank: lockable. Operated by wire pull. Bonnet lock/catch: bonnet catch cable control moved into glove compartment. Engine compartment sealing: moulded rubber sealing (foam rubber). Formerly two-piece lipped seal. Rear hood – model 15: water catch tray altered (necessitated by new oil-bath air filter).
1.8.68	118000001 (111/112) (115/116)	–	Paintwork: Cobalt Blue, Toga White. Continued lines: Regal Red, Chinchilla. Dropped: VW Blue, Lotus White.
	(113/114)	–	New: Cobalt Blue, Peru Green, Diamond Blue, Toga White. Continued lines: Savanna Beige, Regal Red, Chinchilla. Dropped: Delta Green, Zenith Blue, Lotus White, VW Blue.
	(141/144)	–	New: Cyprus Green, Toga White, Oriole Yellow, Sunset, Chrome Blue. Continued lines: Cherry Red. Dropped: Finch Green, Gobi Beige, Velour Red, Chinchilla, Regatta Blue, Lotus White, Bermuda.
	(147)	–	Continued lines: Neptune Blue, Light Grey.
	(151/152)	–	New: Cobalt Blue, Peru Green, Diamond Blue, Toga White. Continued lines: Savanna Beige, Regal Red, Chinchilla. Dropped: Delta Green, Zenith Blue, Lotus White, VW Blue.
15.9.68	119150000	–	Front backrests: inner adjusting cams equipped additionally with retaining bolts and springs.

Year	Chassis No.	Assembly No.	Modification
25.11.68	149431008 (141/142)	–	Cabriolet hood: new detachable rear window (one piece safety glass). Formerly stitched-in Polyglas. Hood catches moved to side roof frame.

Electrics

Year	Chassis No.	Assembly No.	Modification
3.1.68	118443379	–	Hazard warning system 12V: changeover from direction indicators to warning indicators in warning indicator switch. Formerly changeover in flasher relay.
3.4.68	–	122168949	Ignition coil: new high performance ignition coil. Formerly normal coil.
11.4.68	148760153 (141/144)	–	Windscreen wiper motor: now worm drive. Formerly spur gear drive.
7.5.68	118857720 (M88) 118857708 118857872 118856529	DO352113 FI4044775 HO976398 H5327302	Generator and regulating switch: terminals of generator D+ and DF and terminal on regulating switch D+ have screwed connections. Formerly push-on connections.
1.5.68	118799673	–	Distributor: all engines provided with sticker for basic timing setting.
7.6.68	118953664	–	Fused terminal blocks now with push-on plug terminals. Formerly screw terminals.
1.8.68	119000001	–	Direction indicators now with flashing hazard warning system. Warning lights: new warning light windows in instrument and switch buttons identified by symbols. Earth leads: all electrical fittings equipped with earth leads.

General modifications

Year	Chassis No.	Assembly No.	Modification
1.8.68	119000002	–	Volkswagen 1300: now with disc brakes on front axle (M80).
1.8.68	119000008	FI462682	Volkswagen 1300: now fitted with semi-automatic gears (M9).
1.8.68		–	In the USA the Beetle is available also with the combination of manual gear change and double-jointed, trailing-arm rear axle.

1969

The 1500 Beetle has an engine cover with 10 horizontal ventilation louvres. The number of air louvres on the VW Cabrio is increased to 28. The additional louvres are required because the Export Beetle for the USA is fitted with the 1600 Transporter engine (47 bhp).

In the US specification the indicator and rear lights are fitted with side marker lights and reflectors, and in addition with door-open warning buzzer connected to combined steering/ignition lock. A special reflector is bolted on to the bumper bracket for the US models.

Optionally, the 1300/1500 models come with an 'L' package, containing the following luxuries and extras: 2 reversing lights, bumpers with rubber moulding, padded dashboard, anti-dazzle driving mirror, lockable glove compartment lid, make-up mirror in the sun visor, door pocket in passenger door, second ashtray in rear, loop pile carpets. With these additional fittings the models are called the VW 1300 L and VW 1500 L respectively. All Beetle engines have enlarged oil ways, a modified oil pump housing and an oil pressure relief valve. The 1.2 and 1.3 litre engines are fitted with the thermostatically controlled carburettor pre-heat system already fitted to the 1.5 litre engine. Furthermore, they received the air-filter of the 1.3 litre automatic model.

The *Sparkafer* ("Economy Beetle") is also available with 1300 engine and automatic gears. The 1300 is available optionally with a 1.2 litre engine and disc brakes (front).

Dates and facts

1969	Feb.	As a result of the continuing rise of NSU shares up to the level of VW stock, the intention of the Volkswagenwerk AG is announced to amalgamate its subsidiary with the NSU Motorenwerke AG, Neckarsulm.
	11.3.	With the "VW – Porsche Vertriebsgesellschaft mbH" ("the VW – Porsche Marketing Company"), a joint venture between VW and Porsche, a further subsidiary is formed for the sale of Sports cars. The marketing programme includes the VW-Porsche 914(80 bhp), 914/6(110 bhp), and 914/6 Rally (210 bhp).
	May	Building of the sixth domestic Volkswagen factory begins in Salzgitter.
	30.6.	Production of Karmann Ghia Type 34 halted.
	July	In July the magazine Gute Fahrt presents a road-ready Buggy on a Beetle chassis. The firm Karmann takes over manufacture and marketing. The Buggy can be bought as a kit or a complete car. Auto Union GmbH in Ingolstadt halts its assembly of the Beetle for the Wolfsburg parent company. This increases the assembly capacity for Audis. Since May 1965 Audi had built 348,000 Beetles.
	August	Introduction of the new VW 411E with 80 bhp engine and electronic fuel injection. At the same time the VW 181 comes on to the market as multi-purpose vehicle.
	21.8.	Audi and NSU amalgamate into AUDI NSU Auto Union AG. The incorporation of Auto Union GmbH brings the VW share in this company to 59.5%.

132

Engine cover on 1500
Beetle has 10 air louv-
res, Cabrio has 28.

Luxury package: 2 re-
versing lights, bumpers
with rubber moulding.
"VW 1300 L" or "1500
L" badging.

Optional extras for VW 1300 and VW 1500: padded dashboard. Interior door handles and window crank of black plastic. Decorative trim on dashboard dropped. The flaps for the lower heating outlets are operated directly by lever, the remote operation is discontinued.

Chrome silver painted wheels.

Carburettor with thermostatically controlled warm air induction on 1.2 litre and 1.3 litre engines.

134

1969 The most important modifications

Year	Chassis No.	Assembly No.	Modification
Engine/clutch/heating			
1.8.69	1102000001	DO525050	Crankcase: oil circulation
	1102000002	FI778164	changed on 1.2 and 1.6 litre engines.
	1102000003	HI124669	New: two oil pressure valves, diameter
	1102000004	B6000001	of oil channels increased, hub of
			crankshaft pulley lengthened. Drilling
			for cylinder studs on 1.2 litre engine
			increased from 87 to 90 mm.
	1102000005	EO020022	Distributor; 1/1600 M9 + M157. Now
	1102000006	LO024107	with double-action vacuum regulation.
13.8.69	1102061659	AAI895997	Bearing bush for clutch shaft:
	1102058957	AGI895695	upper surface anodized. Formerly
	1102061679	ACI908270	untreated.
	1102059998	AHI902875	
13.9.69	1102163149	AAI987164	Clutch: new: guide shell for return
	1102161389	AB2005650	spring whirl sintered and coated with
15.9.69	1102163923	AC2006070	polyamide.
15.9.69	1102166464	AH1991457	
Fuel system			
1.8.69	1102000001	DO525050	Carburettor pre-heating; warm air
	1102000002	FI778164	taken from right-hand cylinder head.
			Formerly: from left hand heat-exchanger.
	1102000001	DO 525050	Carburettor 28 PICT-2: mixture
	1402000012 (147)	DP 525051	adjusting screw with slimmer cone and
			finer thread pitch, set in a cast housing
			and sealed with a plastic cap.
	1102000001	DO525050	Air filter: intake air pre-heating
	1102000002	FI778164	with thermostat-controlled warm air
			flap operated by Bowden cable.
	1102000002	FI778164	Carburettor 30 PICT-2: now with two
	1102000003	HI124669	mixture adjustment screws. Formerly
			one mixture adjustment screw.
	1102000004	B6000001	Fuel tank system: now with activated
			carbon filter system (California only).
Brakes/wheels/tyres			
1.8.69	1102000001 (1200)	–	Brake system: new dual-circuit system.
	1402014943 (147)	–	
1.8.69	1102000001	–	Warning device for dual-circuit brake

Year	Chassis No.	No.	Modification
			system: tandem brake master cylinder without warning device. Operation of the warning device via two 3-pole brake light switches.

Bodywork

Year	Chassis No.	No.	Modification
1.8.69	110 2 000 003 (1500) 150 2 000 015 (1500) 110 2 000 002 (11/15)	– – –	Engine cover: now with additional air louvres and water drainage tray. Sun visor now no longer swivels to the side for passenger. Luggage compartment at front: lining for luggage bay and instrument panel cover all one piece. Bumpers: in "L-package" (M603) fitted with impact mouldings. Dashboard: trim strips discontinued.
	110 2 000 001 (11/15)	–	Warm air outlets: now with lever on the operating flap. Formerly remote operation. Front wings: drillings for indicator lights modified.
	140 2 000 009 (141-144)	–	Inner wings front and rear: cutouts for indicator and tail lights moved. As a result, head-light pods, rear bumpers, and ram protection at rear (M107) modified.
	110 2 000 001 (except 147)	–	Wheels: now chrome silver painted.
	110 2 000 001 (111/112) (115/116)	– –	Paintwork: new: Pastel White. Continued lines: Regal Red, Chinchilla, Cobalt Blue. Discontinued: Toga White.
	(113/114)	–	New: Elm Green, Pastel White, Clementine.
	(117/118)	–	Continued lines: Savanna Beige, Regal Red, Chinchilla, Cobalt Blue, Diamond Blue. Dropped: Toga White, Peru Green.
	(141/144)	–	New: Bahia Red, Signal Orange, Pampas Yellow, Bright Ivory, Albert Blue, Pastel Blue, Irish Green. Discontinued: Cyprus Green, Toga White, Oriole Yellow, Sunset, Chrome Blue, Cherry Red.
	(147)	–	Continued: Neptune Blue, Light Grey.
	(151/152)	–	New: Elm Green, Pastel White, Clementine. Continued: Savanna Beige, Regal Red, Chinchilla, Cobalt Blue, Diamond Blue. Dropped: Toga White, Peru Green.
16.9.69	110 2159 161 (11.15)	–	Door hinges: hinge pin with two spiral shaped lubrication grooves for multi-purpose grease. Formerly: hinge pin with oil chamber.

Year	Chassis No.	Assembly No.	Modification
Electrics			
1.8.69	110 2 000 001	–	Headlights: new diffusing lens with new approval marking.
	110 2 000 001	–	Indicator and rear lights modified to comply with import regulations in Europe and USA.
	110 2 000 001	–	Steering lock (USA): now with ignition key alarm device. Door contact switch (driver's side) with additional contact for buzzer.
	110 2 000 001	–	Interior light: switch inserted in lens.
	110 2 000 001	–	Warning device for dual-circuit brake system: two 3-pole brake light switches. Formerly: Tandem-brake master cylinder with cast-in housing for warning switch.
	110 2 000 001	–	Windscreen wiper system: now secured with splined cone and cap nut.
	140 2 000 001	–	Speedometer: Surround and trim ring in the dashboard now matt. Formerly bright plated.
12.8.69	110 2 059 477	–	Headlights: new sealing ring between wing and headlight.
14.11.69	140 2 105 984 (147)	–	Reverse lights now with earth lead.
15.12.69	110 2 459 522	–	Indicator light at front: side area of plexi-glass lengthened by 1.5 mm.
General modifications			
1.8.69	110 2 000 001		Chassis No. now 10 digits. Formerly 9 digits.

1970

As a prelude to the new model year VW presents a completely redesigned Beetle model: the VW 1302 with MacPherson strut front suspension and semi-trailing arm rear suspension. The new space-saving MacPherson strut front suspension increase the luggage space from 140 to 260 litres (VDA norm 225 1); the spare wheel is recessed into the floor.

In conjunction with the semi-trailing arm rear suspension familiar in the automatic Beetle, the 1302 Beetle possesses one of the most technically sophisticated chassis of its class. The front bumpers and the front bumper brackets are reinforced. The left-hand rear bumper bracket has a towing eye welded on.

The frame head has a flatter design to accommodate the MacPherson strut front suspension; transverse control arm and stabiliser are secured to it. At the front right a towing eye is welded on.

The greater height of the 1.3 and 1.6 litre engines necessitates a more curved engine lid.

New is the throughflow ventilation (crescent-shaped vents on rear side windows), which in conjunction with the fresh air ventilation (electric fan optional) gives a draught-free ventilation. On the dashboard directional regulators and two further slots in the facia enable a more powerful air-stream to be emitted.

The through-flow ventilation is also available on the VW 1300, but not on the VW 1200.

The new 1302 Beetle can be fitted optionally with three engines of different performance; namely, 1302 with 34 or 44 bhp engine, and 1302S with new 1.6 litre engine and 50 bhp. The new compression ratio (7.5) enables the redesigned 1.3 litre unit to achieve 44 bhp. The 1.6 litre engine has, like the redesigned 1.3 litre unit, double inlet ports and an oil cooler shifted further forward with its own cooling air flow. An additional thermostat installed in the oil bath air filter controls the warm air flow to the carburettor.

A new ignition/starter switch ensures that when the ignition is turned off the headlights are also automatically turned off.

Since the new model year there are practically two distinct Beetle lines. The old lineage with the 1200 and 1300 models, and the new line with the 1302 and 1302 S models – see also Model overview.

Dates and facts

1970	The largest Rent-a-car company, Selbstfahrer – Union (Self-drive Union) is taken over by Volkswagen.
8.7.	The one millionth VW rolls off the line at the Brazilian factory, daily production stands at 970 VWs. Managing Director is Rudolf Leiding. The market share in Brazil is 61.2 per cent for private cars, 49 per for Transporters.
Sept.	The VW K70 passenger car, produced by NSU engineers and brought into mass production by Volkswagen, is presented to the public; production begins in autumn at the newly built Salzgitter factory.

Dates and facts

Aug. The Volkswagen achieves its highest turnover in England since first exporting there in 1953: 41,706 units (24,057). The VW market share in England rises to 3.5 per cent for private cars and 1.9 per cent for Transporters. There are 262 VW dealers under the direction of VW Motors (Thomas Tilling Group). Beetle price in England £684 to £699.

In mid-September at Audi NSU in Neckarsulm, the one millionth NSU car since production recommenced rolls off the line in 1958 (an Ro 80).

VW 1302: New front end. Running boards, wings, both hoods modified. Through-flow ventilation.

The increased height of the 1.3 and 1.6 litre engines necessitates a more sharply curved engine cover.

VW 1302: through-flow ventilation in rear side panel.

VW 1302: Luggage capacity under the bonnet raised from 140 to 260 litres as result of new MacPherson strut suspension. Front closing panel lowered. Bumpers and brackets strengthened. The spare wheel is recessesd under floor of luggage compartment.

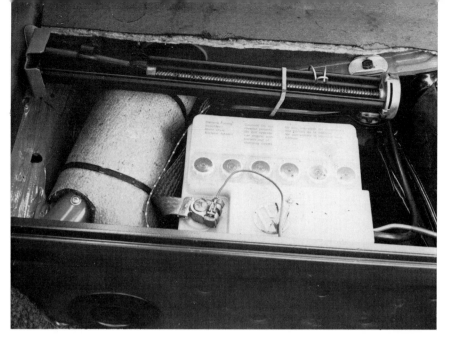

Jack stored underneath rear seat.

Two additional air louvres in the dashboard, so-called *Mann-Anströmer* (personal vents).

VW 1302: MacPherson strut suspension with frame head, control arms and stabiliser. Safety worm and roller steering.

MacPherson strut front
suspension with
transverse control arms
and stabiliser.

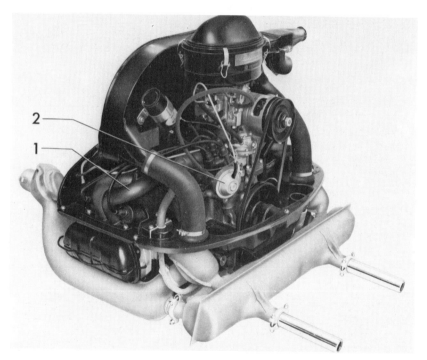

1.6 litre engine/50 bhp
with twin inlet manifold
(1) and double acting
vacuum control (2).

2

1

VW 1302: semi-trailing
arm rear axle fitted as
standard, as used on the
automatic Beetle since
1967.

142

VW 1300: old Beetle shape. Engine hood as on VW 1302 with 10 ventilation louvres. Through flow ventilation in rear side panels.

1.3 and 1.6 litre engines: oil-cooler made from sheet aluminium with coupling flange moved further forward.

Additional thermostat in oil bath air filter.

Left: single port cylinder head. Right: double port cylinder head for 1.3 and 1.6 litre engines from August 1970.

1970 Beetles	VW 1200	VW 1300	VW 1302	VW 1302S	VW 1302 LS Cabrio
Bodywork	old shape	old shape	new shape with larger luggage compartment	new shape with larger luggage compartment	new shape with larger luggage compartment
Chassis	old front axle rear swing axle without compensating spring	old front axle rear swing axle with compensatimg spring	new front axle double-jointed rear axle	new front axle double-jointed rear axle	new front axle double-jointed rear axle
Engine	1200/34 HP optionally 1300/44 HP	1300/44 HP optionally 1200/34 HP	1300/44 HP optionally 1200/34 HP	1600/50 HP	1600/50 HP
Brakes	dual-circuit front & rear drums	dual-circuit front & rear drums	dual-circuit front & rear drums optional front discs	dual-circuit front discs rear drums	dual-circuit front discs rear drums
Top speed	115 km/h	125 km/h	125 km/h	135 km/h	130 km/h
Weight	unladen 760 kg full 1140 kg trailer limit 650 kg	unladen 820 kg full 1200 kg trailer limit 650 kg	unladen 870 kg full 1270 kg trailer limit 650 kg	unladen 870 kg full 1270 kg trailer limit 650 kg	unladen 920 kg full 1280 kg trailer limit 650 kg
Price/DM	4695	5495	5745	5945	7490

On the German market semi-automatic transmission with double-jointed rear axle is available for all models, even for the 'Economy Beetle'; this combination is not, however, available with the 1200 engine. The top speed with automatic transmission is quoted 5 km/h lower by the factory. In the well-known 'L-package' (2 reversing lights, rubber inserts on bumpers, carpeted floor, door pocket on right, second ashtry in rear, anti-dazzle driving mirror, make-up mirror, padded dashboard, brake warning lights, lock for glove compartment), the two-speed fresh air blower is now included. Cars with L-package have an additional 'L' added to motif on engine hood.

For the USA, in addition to the new Volkswagen models, there is also a custom model available with oil shape bodywork, double-joint rear axle, drum brakes and 1600 engine.

1970   The most important modifications

Year	Chassis No.	Assembly No.	Modification
Engine/clutch/heating			
1.8.70	111 2000 002 111 2000 003 111 2000 008	ABO 000 001 ADO 000 001 AEO 000 001	Cluch release bearing: new axially guided release bearing. Clutch: now without release ring, torsion spring modified.
	111 2000 003 111 2000 008 111 2000 010	ADO 000 001 AEO 000 001 AFO 000 001	Crankcase: now of more heat-resistant material (AS-41)

Year	Chassis No.	Assembly No.	Modification
	111 2000 009	ACO 000 001	1.3 and 1.6 litre engines now with compression ratio 6.6:1 for petrol with low octane level.
	111 2000 010	AFO 000 010	
	111 2000 002	ABO 000 001	V-belt: now stretch-resistant.
	111 2000 003	ADO 000 001	
	181 2000 007	AGO 000 001	
	111 2000 008	AEO 000 001	
	111 2000 009	ACO 000 001	
	111 2000 010	AFO 000 001	
1.9.70	111 2082 957	DO 681 001	Rocker covers now with retaining lugs for gaskets.
	111 2082 958	ABO 035 142	
	111 2082 959	ADO 029 897	
	111 2082 960	AEO 044 772	
	181 2082 961	AGO 000 238	
	111 2080 962	ACO 000 187	
	111 2082 963	AFO 000 149	
12.9.70	111 2148 684 (1600)	–	Ignition coil, distributor: modified rubber protective caps.
30.9.70	111 2174 804	ABO 060 950	Gasket for left-hand pre-heating pipe: opening 19 mm bore. Formerly 6 mm bore.
	111 2174 902	ADO 059 694	
6.10.70	111 2186 917	AFO 000 155	
8.10.70	111 2190 819	ACO 000 323	
6.10.70	111 2184 833 (16000)	–	Dynamo: new washers on terminals, cable eyes with rubber protective caps.
26.11.70	111 2342 211 (1600)	–	Dynamo: upper carbon brush window covered.

Fuel system

Year	Chassis No.	Assembly No.	Modification
2.1.70	110 2473 154	DO 592 446	Idling cut-off valve: steel casing. Formerly brass.
	110 2473 155	FI 932 909	
	110 2473 156	HI 187 830	
	110 2473 157	B6 192 533	
	110 2473 158	EO 020 938	
	110 2473 159	LO 024 788	
2.1.70	110 2473 154	DO 592 446	Stop for stepped cam of automatic choke; new steel dowel pin. Formerly steel grooved pin.
	110 2473 155	FI 932 909	
	110 2473 156	HI 187 830	
	110 2473 158	EO 020 938	
	110 2473 159	LO 024 788	
13.1.70	110 2528 697	–	Petrol tank now secured by clamp plates with rounded corners.
1.8.70	111 2000 002	ABO 000 001	Oil bath air filter: now with thermostat. Formerly with Bowden cable.
	111 2000 003	ADO 000 001	
	111 2000 008	AEO 000 001	
	111 2000 010	AFO 000 001	
	111 2000 001 (1302)	–	Filler cap: screw thread. Formerly bayonet cap.

Year	Chassis No.	No.	Modification
			Fuel system: new breather with trap valve.
	111 2000 001	DO 675 001	Carburettor 30, 31, 34 PICT-3: now
	111 2000 002	ABO 000 001	with by-pass drilling and by-pass
	111 2000 003	ADO 000 001	mixture cut-off valve, and
	181 2000 007	AGO 000 001	without electromagnetic cut-off
	111 2000 008	AEO 000 001	valve.
	111 2000 009	ACO 000 001	
	111 2000 010	AFO 000 001	
17.9.70	111 2156 331	ABO 045 198	Carburettor 31 PICT-3: new: main jet x 145, air correction jet 170z, idle jet 60z, idle air jet 120.
	111 2158 703	AEO 058 480	Emission control system (M157): new throttle valve with closing damper for manual transmission vehicles.
29.9.70	111 2026 187	–	Filler cap for petrol tank: thread length 41 mm. Formerly 37 mm.

Front axle/steering

Year	Chassis No.	No.	Modification
1.8.70	111 2000 011 (1302) 111 2000 012 (13025)	– –	Front axle: MacPherson strut axle with enlarged drum brakes (248 mm diameter). Formerly ball joint axle. New: MacPherson strut axle with disc brakes (1302S). Steering: now with control arms. Tie rod ends now with increased radial elasticity.
1.8.70	111 2000 001 (1200) 111 2000 002 (1300) 141 2000 004	– – –	Steering: steering column and bolting modified. Steering column-mounted switch shortened.
16.11.70	111 2325 213	2 792 995	Front axle beam now with towing eye.

Rear axle/gears

Year	Chassis No.	No.	Modification
1.8.70	111 2000 003	–	Semi-trailing arm suspension: now single spring plates. Formerly double spring plates.

Brakes/wheels/tyres

Year	Chassis No.	No.	Modification
1.8.70	111 2000 011 (1302)	–	Tandem-brake master cylinder: new: one outlet for front brake circuit with T-piece. Formerly two outlets. Front brakes: drum brake now 248 mm diameter.
	111 2000 012 (13025)	–	Front brakes: disc brake with backplate changed in shape, as a result of which cooling is improved.

Year	Chassis No.	Assembly No.	Modification
6.2.70	110 2619 133	–	Heating lever: now cranked beneath the knob and shortened by 10 mm.
22.6.70	110 3032 778 (right-hand drive)	–	Clutch pedal travel now limited by stop behind tread plate.
1.8.70	111 2000 001 (1302)	–	Frame head: to accommodate Mac-Pherson strut suspension, flatter T-shaped construction. Clutch and brake pedals: now positioned more vertically. Distance between accelerator and brake pedal 60 mm. Formerly 80 mm.

Bodywork

Year	Chassis No.	Assembly No.	Modification
24.2.70	140 2572 520	–	Rear window: now with heater.
6.5.70	140 2758 569 (143/144)	–	Rear window: heater outlets discontinued.
1.8.70	141 2000 004	–	Operation of footwell heating: now by lever on operating flap. Formerly remote operation. Towing: new towing hook bolted to left rear bumper bracket.
	141 2000 004	–	Door locking: now incorporated in
	151 2000 005	–	interior release.
	(15)	–	Warm air system: warm air outlets modified (necessitated by lengthened front end).
	(15)	–	Engine hood now more sharply curved. Water drainage tray discontinued (only on 1.6 engine).
			Dashboard: two additional air louvres.
	(15)	–	Ventilation: two-speed fresh air blower.
	(11/m121)		
	(11,15)	–	Tank filler flap and operation: now retained with locking pin. Formerly: retained by locking hook.
	111 2000 002	–	Engine hood: now more sharply curved. Front seats: backrest sides wider. New: guide rails on floorpan of 'T' section. Formerly 'U' section. Guide rail on seat frame modified accordingly.
	111 2000 001 (111/112) (115/116)	–	Paintwork: new: Clementine, Marina Blue, Kansas Beige. Continued: Pastel White. Dropped: Regal Red, Cobalt Blue, Chinchilla.
	(113/114)	–	New: Sapphire Blue, Marina Blue, Iberian Red.

Year	Chassis No.		Assembly No.	Modification
		(117/118)		Shantung Yellow, Kansas Beige, Silver Metallic, Colorado Metallic, Gemini Metallic. Continued: Pastel White, Elm Green, Clementine. Dropped: Savanna Beige, Regal Red, Chinchilla, Cobalt Blue, Diamond Blue.
		(141/144)	–	New: Adriatic Blue, Blood Orange, Lemon Yellow, Meadow Green. Continued: Bright Ivory, 'Bahia' Red, Signal Orange, Irish Green. Dropped: Albert Blue, Pampas Green, Pastel Blue.
		(147)	–	Continued: Neptune Blue, Light Grey.
		(151/152)	–	New: Sapphire Blue, Marina Blue, Iberian Red, Shantung Yellow, Kansas Beige. Continued: Pastel White, Elm Green, Clementine. Dropped: Savanna Beige, Regal Red, Chinchilla, Cobalt Blue, Diamond Blue.
		1112000002 1512000002	–	Front end of VW 1302: modified as result of new MacPherson strut suspension (74 mm longer). Bumpers: sheet metal thickness 1.75 mm. Formerly 1.5 mm. Towing eyes – VW 1302: welded onto frame head right and on to left rear bumper bracket. Ventilation: new fresh air system with through-flow ventilation.

Electrics

Year	Chassis No.		Assembly No.	Modification
1.8.70	1112000001		–	Fuse box: now with relay board. On VW 1302 installed on left beside steering column.
	1112000011	(1302)	–	Sender for fuel gauge: sender transmitter with two float arms of differing lengths. Formerly one float arm.
	1112000008		–	Tail light (USA): new: enlarged light lenses. Enlarged reflector inserts Type 1.
	1112000001		–	Windscreen wash: new design like Type 4 with compressed air feed pipe from spare wheel for windscreen wash container.
25.11.70	1112339482		ADO105510	Dynamo: sheet metal cover for
25.11.70	1112342211		AEO166832	upper carbon brush window.

1971

The contours of the engine lid have slightly changed, and it now has a total of 26 air louvres (except on *Sparkäfer* ('Economy Beetle') for improved engine cooling.

The water drainage tray underneath the cooing air louvres has been discontinued. For this reason, the generator, distributor, ignition coil and spark plugs are better protected against the wet.

The rear window is 4 cm larger and affords easier rear vision. New interior features are principally the new safety steering wheel with deformable Section and enlarged centre pad; also the steering column mounted (left) wash-wipe lever.

The rear luggage space has a collapsible shelf. On the rear wheel arches sound proofing material is fitted.

The through-flow ventilation behind the side windows is fitted with a one-way flap, to prevent draughts when the windows are open, and to prevent water penetrating inside through the vents.

For increased safety in a collision all Beetle models have a screw threaded tank filler cap with provision against overtightening.

For swifter control of the air flap in the air filter intake this is controlled via a vacuum capsule with bimetal spring.

A diagnosis plug in the engine bay enables the garage to check automatically a number of inspection points with a computer.

The dual diaphragm vacuum unit on the distributor is dropped, and is replaced by a single vacuum unit.

The small Ghia model is fitted with the stronger bumpers from the Beetle and the very large rear lights of the VW 1600.

Dates and facts

1971 Feb.   As a restructuring of its Austrian Import Branch the Volkswagenwerk AG in Wolfsburg founds Volkswagen Import Austria in Vienna, in which Porsche Konstruktionen KG of Salzburg has a 75 per cent share (formerly general importer) and VW Wolfsburg 25 per cent. For Audi-NSU sales to Austria, Audi-NSU Austria GmbH and Co. KG Vienna is formed (VW 75 per cent, Piëch family 25 per cent). Concentration of the Audi and NSU head operations in Ingolstadt. After the strike in Autumn and the breakthrough of the NSU-models, a loss of 34.9 million DM is recorded which the VW Organvertrag takes over. In Wankel licences Audi-NSU takes 23.6 million DM, of which the shareholders each receive 6.26 DM = 10.9 million DM.

2.7.   The experimental safety car (ESVW1) announced by Volkswagen in October 1970 is first shown to the public as a prototype. The vehicle is not to be put into mass production.

27.8.   The 5,000,000th Volkswagen is shipped to the USA.

1.10.   After the departure of Prof. Dr. Lotz, Rudolf Leiding takes over the running of the corporation as a whole, as Chairman of the Board of Management of Volkswagenwerk AG.
Volkswagen Brussels is founded, in which Volkswagenwerk AG has a 75 per cent share. Assembly capacity amounts to 800 vehicles per working day from a workforce of 2600.

The rear window is extended at top by 4 cm.

150

The engine hood has slightly modified contours and a total of 26 air louvres.

Luggage compartment with removable cover (except VW 1200).

Interior ventilation is improved by means of three separate ventilation slots in the rear.

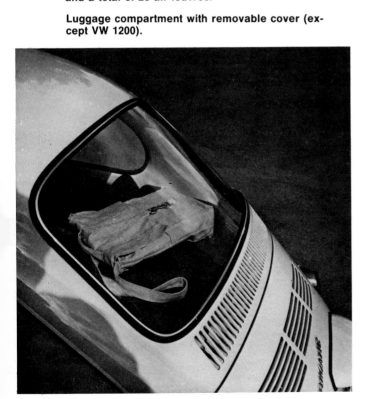

Safety steering wheel with large centre pad (except VW 1200).

Right of the steering wheel:
Lever for windscreen wiper and washer.

For automated inspection:
Diagnosis plug in engine bay.

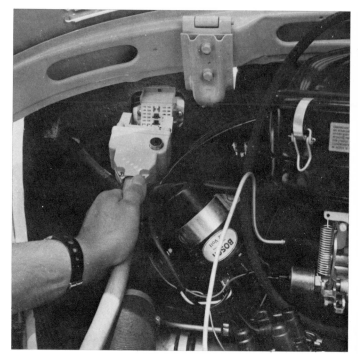

Air filter with temperature and vacuum-controlled
intake air pre-heating.

VW 1300: engine hood with 26 air louvres.

152

1971 The most important modifications

Year	Chassis No.	Assembly No.	Modification
Engine/clutch/heating			
12.2.71	1112580353	AF0000293	Pulley: new marking of TDC.
15.2.71	1112596148	AE0284764	
16.2.71	1112593681	AB0176699	
	1112596492	AC0000848	
	1112594955	AD0178486	
18.2.71	1112598841	DO735269	
26.2.71	1812617472	AG0001545	
1.3.71	1112669688	–	Spark plugs: now Champion L88A plugs. Formerly L88.
9.3.71	1112688024	DO746684	Pistons and cylinders: now two combination sizes. Formerly. three combination sizes.
	1112689929	AB0208118	
11.3.71	1112690596	AD0200020	
12.3.71	1112698340	AE0330184	
28.4.71	1112823698	AD0236134	Oil pump: gear wheels 26 mm wide, required oil level increased. Formerly gear wheels 21 mm wide. Camshaft: adapted to the modified pump. (M 819 – angled drive)
	1112823926	AE0395938	
29.4.71	1112830896	AD0236195	
30.4.71	1112835249	AE0397119	
7.5.71	1112846540	AF0000399	
1.8.71	1122000002	AB0350001	
	1122000010	AC0003240	
15.6.71	1112920875	AB0313346	Distributor; now single vacuum take-off, Formerly double vacuum.
1.8.71	1122000002	AB0350001	Distributor: now with single vacuum take-off, ignition timing changed. Formerly: double vacuum take-off.
	1122000003	AD0360023	
	1822000007	AG0003001	
	1122000010	AC0003240	
	1122000008	AE0558001	Ignition system: distributor and ignition timing adapted to the extended exhaust emission regulations.
	1122000009	AH0000001	
	1122000008	AE0558001	Compression: reduced to 7.3 from 7.5 by changes in the pistons and cylinder heads.
	1122000009	AH0000001	
	1122000002	AB0350001	Intake manifold pre-heating at exhaust: now from left to right. Formerly from right to left.
	1122000003	AD0360023	
	1122000008	AE0558001	
	1122000009	AH0000001	
	1122000010	AC0003240	
	1122000011	AF0000445	
	1122000002 (1300)	–	Ignition coil, distributor: modified rubber protection caps. Generator: new washers under terminals. Cable eyes with rubber protection caps. New: upper carbon brush window covered.

Year	Chassis No.	Assembly No.	Modification
1.9.71	1122073652	AA3978108	Clutch release-bearing: clutch release spindle 20 mm dia. Formerly: 16 mm dia.
4.10.71	1122131717	AB0383315	
5.10.71	1122132974	D0845245	
6.10.71	1122133730	AD0317989	
7.10.71	1122199612	AE0626192	
11.10.71	1122137213	AH0001279	
12.10.71	1122205780	AC0004237	
15.10.71	1122212134	AF0000570	
12.10.71	1122206303	AE0627299	Throttle positioner discontinued.

Fuel system

Year	Chassis No.	Assembly No.	Modification
2.2.71	1112526082 (1302)	–	Sealing for tank filler cap: new lip seal. Formerly O-ring.
1.3.71	1112669689	AB0193791	Carburettor 31 PICT-3: stepped cam marked with code 37. Formerly 47.
15.6.71	1112920875	AB0313346	Carburettor 30, 31, 34 PICT-3:
	1122000010	AC0003240	new: retard take off for
	1122000011	AF0000445	ignition timing on carburettor discontinued (except USA & Canada)
1.8.71	1122000003 (1302)	–	Fuel tank: now with baffle.
1.8.71	1122000002	AB0350001	
	1122000003	AD0360023	
	1822000007	AG0003001	
	1122000008	AE0558001	
	1122000009	AH0000001	
	1122000010	AC0003240	
	1122000011	AF0000445	
1.8.71	1122000009	AH0000001	Emission control system: recirculation of exhaust gas (only USA, California).

Front axle/steering

Year	Chassis No.	Assembly No.	Modification
20.4.71	1112810528 (1302)	–	Securing flange of shock absorbers now 9.5 mm thick. Formerly 7.5 mm thick.

Rear axle/gears

Year	Chassis No.	Assembly No.	Modification
19.1.71	1112485954	–	Double-joint shaft: joint gaiters retained between two beads on the shaft. Formerly secured by two ear clamps.
14.7.71	1113115295	BE0424988	Gearbox casing now with oil drain screw. Gasket increased in thickness from 0.75 mm to 1.5 mm.

Year	Chassis No.		Assembly No.	Modification
3.9.71	1122073652 1122073642 1122073645 1122073077		AA3978108 AB3945927 AM3957400 AH3957300	Clutch operation: operation modified, giving increased efficiency on disengagement of clutch. Longer clutch lever.

Chassis

25.8.71	1122005693		–	Hand brake lever: push button 7 mm longer, rubber grommet discontinued.
3.9.71	1122076199		–	Gearshift: new 3-point location for gearlever and lateral guide for stop plate. Formerly 4-point system.

Bodywork

1.8.71	1122000001 1522000005	(11)	–	Rear window: height increased by 40 mm
		(11/15)	–	Rear hood: lock secured with one bolt. Formerly 3 fastening bolts. 4 sets of cooling-air louvres (except 1200). Formerly 2 sets of cooling air louvres. Water drainage tray discontinued (1.3 litre engine).
		(11)	–	Through-flow ventilation: left and right of rear view window 3 ventilation slots with one-way flaps. Formerly 2 ventilation slots on each side without flaps.
		(11)	–	Rear luggage space: now with shelf (except 1200). Door fittings: outside door handle with longer trigger (therefore, deeper recess in door outer panel); door lock and striker plate modified.
	1122000001 1522000005 1422000004		– –	Fastening of body to frame: fixing support on rear side panel modified. Bumpers: design now as on Type 3. Bumper brackets modified. Bodywork: side panels and valances front and rear adapted to accommodate modified bumpers. Roof modified. Doors adapted to suit new roof. New window glass, triggers and outside door handles, locks and striker plates. Fastening of bodywork to frame: fixing support on side panel modified.

Year	Chassis No.		Assembly No.	Modification
	1422000004	(143/144)	–	Uprights between side and door windows: now welded into roof and side panel. Formerly bolted. Dashboard: new: covered with matt-black trim material. Fresh-air controls relocated beneath radio aperture. External mirror: modified casing. Seats: darts sewn in cross-wise. Formerly lengthwise. Lower sections of seats with cloth trim.
	1122000001		–	Seal between frame and bodywork now foam rubber. Formerly rubber moulding seal.
	1122000001	(111/112)	–	Paintwork: new: Brilliant Orange, Texas Yellow. Continued: Pastel White, Marina Blue. Dropped: Clementine, Kansas Beige.
		(115/116)	–	
		(113/114)	–	New: 'Kasan' Red, Amber Texas Yellow, Sumatra Green, Gentian Blue, Turquoise-Metallic. Continued: Pastel White, Marina Blue, Kansas Beige, Silver-Metallic, Colorado-Metallic, Gemini Metallic. Dropped: Sapphire Blue, Iberian Red, Shantung Yeoolw, Elm Green, Clementine.
		(117/118)		
		(141-144)	–	New: Saturn Yellow, Silver-Metallic, Gold-Metallic, Gemini-Metallic. Continued: 'Bahia' Red, Bright Ivory, Signal Orange, Irish Green. Dropped: lemon Yellow.
		(147)	–	Continued: Neptune Blue, Light Grey.
		(151/152)	–	New: 'Kasan' Red, Amber, Texas Yellow, Sumatra Green, Gentian Blue, Silver Metallic, Colorado Metallic, Turquoise Metallic, Gemini Metallic. Continued: Pastel White, Marina Blue, Kansas Beige. Dropped: Sapphire Blue, Iberian Red, Shantung Yellow, Elm Green, Clementine.
	1122000001 1522000005	(113-118)	–	Rear seat: secured with catch hook on seat frame and strap attached to luggage compartment floor.
12.11.71	112232498	(113,114) (117, 118)	–	Front seats: padding with approximately 20 mm foam inlay.
12.11.71	1122266171		–	Rear guide for crank-operated window: new: cover plate for door lock discontinued.
6.12.71	1122389435		–	Bonnet: rubber insert between top of bonnet lock and bonnet. Formerly without insert.

Year	Chassis No.	Assembly No.	Modification

Electrics

Year	Chassis No.		Assembly No.	Modification
1.8.71	1122000001		–	Fuse box: new: with X-terminal. Instruments: new: Gearing of speedometer adjusted to take into account the different tyre sizes. Notation modernised, end of scale increased.
	112200002	(1302)	–	Steering column stalk switch now with windscreen wiper switch (additional function: single wipe). Windscreen wiping system: new: internal switching of wiper motor modified. Intermittent and dry wipe as optional extra.

157

1972

In February of this year a 1302S marks the Beetle's greatest triumph since production began. With 15,007,034 vehicles produced it overtakes the Model T Ford to become the 'World Champion'.

From August the VW 1303 rolls off the production lines, with a sharply curved windscreen ('Panorama Beetle'). The rear of the Beetle is dominated by large round tail lights, which are mounted on slightly reshaped wings. With the forward shifted windscreen, the roof and the scuttle are moved a good way forward. The bonnet is shorter as a result, and now comes without the VW symbol. The door opening angle can now be increased to 90 degrees.

The Beetle Cabrio matches the new VW 1300 in appearance. The vehicles with a short front, the 'Economy' Beetle (1200/34 bhp) and the VW 1300 (44 bhp) remain in the series. The Panorama Beetle comes in two engine versions: with 1.3 litre engine/44 bhp and 1.6 engine/50 bhp. In relation to its predecessor the VW 1300 is 20 kg heavier.

The interior has a new padded dashboard, with improved ventilation and large deformable surfaces. Directly behind the windscreen is a heating and fresh air channel running crosswise over the whole width of the interior, with 42 air louvres, flanked additionally on the left and right defroster nozzles from the side window.

The pull-knob for opening the tank flap is discontinued; the bonnet is opened by a lever, which is accommodated as before in the glove compartment.

The fusebox is located underneath the middle of the dashboard and is easily accessible.

The seat subframe consists of a stable three-legged structure, anchored to the chassis tunnel. The adjustment scale of the new safety seats is increased by 6 cm, and the seats can be adjusted into 77 different positions.

With the increased seat adjustment capability, the handbrake lever and gearstick are moved closer to the driver.

In November the carburettor is fitted with a thermostat for the accelerator pump. The oil bath air filter is replaced by a dry air filter with paper element (except VW 1200).

| 1972 | 17.2. | As 'World Champion' the 15,007,034th Beetle rolls off the production line. This beats the previous production record held by the Model T Ford. |

August — As replacement model for the VW 411E, the VW 412E with modified front and rear is brought out.

The Transporter is now available with automatic transmission.

At a Symposium "Electric Road Travel" the prototype of the Volkswagen-Elektromobil is shown for the first time time as a pick-up truck – developed in collaboration with Varta and the Rhein-Westphalia Electrical Company (RWE).

In union with the Yugoslav Volkswagen Import Co. UNIS, Volkswagen builds in Sarajevo an assembly site for vehicles and spare parts production.

24.10. In the Kassel factory the 3 millionth exchange engine is manufactured.

More than 5,000 VW Beetles, each with 5,115 individual parts, are manufactured daily.

VW 1303 with sharply curved windscreen. Roof and scuttle are moved further forward, resulting in a shortened bonnet. The bonnet lock is fitted with a black push button.

VW 1303: fully redesigned dashboard. Fresh air channel across the whole width of the vehicle. Fusebox in the centre of the dashboard. Knob for tank flap discontinued. Defroster nozzles on left and right.

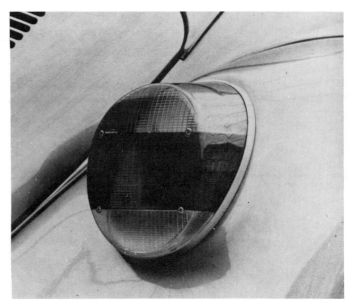

VW1303: Large 3-section lights on the rear mud-guard ('Elephants' feet').

Lever for unlocking bonnet in glove compartment.

On 17.2.1972 in Wolfsburg the Beetle is hailed as World Champion. With over 15 million units it beats the previous production record held by the Model T Ford.

Dry air filter with paper element.

Sliding steel roof in mass production with wind deflector. On official VW photos the VW symbol is still shown on the bonnet; the 1303, however, is put into mass production without it.

Three-rail seats. Seat adjusters on the central tunnel.

Cutaway picture of the 1303 Beetle.

1972 The most important modifications

Year	Chassis No.	Assembly No.	Modification
Engine/clutch/heating			
10.1.72	1122429477	–	Guide tube for accelerator cable: ends of guide tube sealed with plugs.
24.3.72	1122670583 (1200)	–	Clutch release bearing: centrally carried ball bearing. Formerly carbon release ring.
16.6.72	1122927493	AB633668	Cover piece for crankshaft pulley now discontinued.
	1122929313	AE902742	
	1122929558	AD530106	
20.6.72	1122933968	AG009343	Oil strainer cap: drain plug and washer discontinued.
27.6.72	1122957000	AF000764	
	1122939405	AC005994	
	1122943471	AE898985	
28.6.72	1122944804	AB632352	
29.6.72	1122947386	AD530013	
3.7.72	1122952726	AH005321	
5.7.72	1122957069	DO977392	
1.8.72	1132071860	DO993590	Rocker arms now as in 1.3 and 1.6 engines.
1.8.72	1132000002	AB699001	Crankcase ventilation: vent pipe from oil filler with rubber valve discontinued.
	1132000019	AC006001	
	1132000024	AH020001	
	1132000003	AD598001	
	1832000010	AG011001	
	1832000010	AG011001	
	1132000030	AF000801	
	1132000001	AE917264	
	1132000003	AD598001	Clutch: new diaphragm spring clutch. Formerly coil spring clutch.
	1832000010	AG011001	
	1132000011	AE917264	
	1132000012	AH005900	
	1132000020	AF000801	
21.8.72	1132095992	DO992261	Pistons: new domed pistons with compression ratio 7.3:1. Formerly flat pistons with compression ratio 7.0:1.
1.9.72	2132014587	AD626466	Cylinder head stud: new M8 (ductile stud) with threaded insert. Formerly M10 (tensile stud).
7.9.72	2132014914	AF032871	
5.12.72	1132376816	AD719066	
6.12.72	1132382821	AK041902	
11.12.72	1132382872	AH037887	
12.12.72	1132390253 (M9)	AH053012	
10.11.72	1132302030	AB785890	Exhaust valve: oil deflector ring discontinued.
	1132302031	AH033862	
	1132304614	AK023475	

Year	Chassis No.	Assembly No.	Modification
Fuel system			
1.3.72	1122581695	AB0530394	Fuel pump with pressed casing: now
7.3.72	1122639727	AE0793575	with built-in cut-off valve.
8.3.72	1122644302	AD0468330	Formerly: fuel pump and cut-off
13.3.72	1122639728	AH0004174	valve separate.
6.3.72	1122636	–	Temperature control for air filter: new dual control. Formerly single control.
4.5.72	1122818748	–	Activated carbon filter system: new polyamide connecting pipes 11 or 12 mm bore. Formerly metal Mecano-Bundy tubes.
25.9.72	1132196230	AB747704	Carburettor 31 PICT-4; new thermostat for accelerator pump. Air filter: new dry air filter with paper element. Formerly: oil bath air filter.
23.11.72	1132362151	AK033542	Float for carburettor 30 PICT-3 now of foam. Formerly hollow float.
Front axle/steering			
23.2.72	1122509832 (1302)	–	Steering stop: repositioned stop on steering gear. Formerly on bearing block for steering arm.
1.8.72	1132075826 (1200)	–	Axle and steering joints: sealing plugs, lubrication orifices and tapped holes discontinued.
Rear axle/transmission			
27.4.72	1122767602	–	Joint protection boots for constant velocity joints: joint protection boot ends enclosed in protective caps. Formerly secured with hose clips.
30.6.72	1122857574	BG0481384	Temperature warning device: now without temperature switch. Formerly, with switch.
7.11.72	1132297984	A02112	Gear ratios 1st and reverse gear: 1st gear 3.78, reverse gear 3.79. Formerly: 1st gear 3.80, reverse gear 3.80.
7.11.72	1132297983 (1300) 1132300195 (1200)	AM02112 AB02112	4th gear ratio now 0.931. Formerly: 0.883.
Brakes/wheels/tyres			
24.1.72	1122471100 (WOB)	–	Pressed steel wheels (except 14, 147,
1.2.72	1522363628	–	181): $4^1/_2$ J x 15 (34 mm offset), only in
4.2.72	1122497034 Emden	–	conjunction with M 170 and USA Series.
		–	Formerly: 4 J x 15 (40 mm offset).

Year	Chassis No.	Assembly No.	Modification
			Tyres (except 14, 147, 181): 6.00 x 15 (M170 and USA series). Formerly: 5.60 x 15.
15.5.72	1122837179 (Teves)	–	Brake master cylinder now without residual pressure valve.
9.6.72	1122923294 (Schafer)	–	
21.6.72	1122931906	–	Pressed steel wheels now centre location. Formerly: location by wheel bolts.
1.8.72	1132000020	–	Rear wheel brakes (M86): new self-adjusting drum brake.
3.8.72	1432096866	–	Tyres: 6.00–15L 4 PR. Formerly 5.60 S–154 PR. Pressed steel wheels: 4½ J x 15. Formerly 4 J x 15.

Chassis

Year	Chassis No.	Assembly No.	Modification
10.1.72	1422249984 (147)	–	Clutch pedal: now with stop: Guide tube for accelerator cable: new: end of guide tube sealed with plug.
10.1.72	1122429477	–	
8.2.72	1122540929	–	Fuel pipe: new: outlet moved to the right side of the frame head. Formerly: outlet above.
1.8.72	1132000001 (except 147)	–	Gear lever: new: cut-out section in frame moved back 40 mm. Gear stick shortened accordingly.
21.11.72	1132360845	–	Brake cable: now 12 wire strands. Formerly: 19.

Bodywork

Year	Chassis No.	Assembly No.	Modification
26.1.72	1522363626 (except USA)	–	Hood fabric: new colour Texas Brown.
28.1.72	1422363608 except USA		
13.6.72	1122875100	–	Roof lining now extending from windscreen to rear window. Formerly only as far as rear window surround.
1.8.72	1132031720 (Emden)	–	Warm air hose between heat exchanger and body now with noise suppression. Formerly metal articulated tube.
1.8.72	1332000004 1532000008	–	New VW 1303 (model modification e.g. new front end, modified interior). Formerly VW 1302.
	1132000001 (113/117) (117/118) (113,135/136)		Paintwork: new: Biscay Blue, Maya Metallic, Alaska Metallic, Marathon Metallic. Continued lines: Amber, Sumatra Green, Turqouise Green. Dropped: Pastel White, Marina Blue, Kansas Beige, Gentian Blue, Silver Metallic, Colorado Metallic, Gemini Metallic.

Year	Chassis No.	Assembly No.	Modification
	(141-144)	–	New: Sun Yellow, Phoenix Red, Olympia Blue, Zambezi Green, Ravenna Green, Marathon Metallic, Alaska Metallic, Saturn Yellow Metallic. Continued lines: Bright Ivory, Saturn Yellow, Signal Orange, Bahia Red.
	(147)	–	Continued lines; Neptune Blue, Light Grey.
	1132000001	–	Front seats: new: three-rail seat.
	(151/152)	–	New: Sun Yellow, Phoenix Red, Olympia Blue, Zambezi Green, Ravenna Green, Marathon metallic, Saturn Yellow metallic. Continued lines: Bright Ivory, Saturn Yellow, Signal Orange, Bahia Red. Dropped: Pastel White, Marina Blue, Kansas Beige.

Electrics

Year	Chassis No.	Assembly No.	Modification
1.8.72	1332000004 (1303)	–	Windscreen wiper system: adapted to revised installation. Dashboard: new inset with rocker switches and controls. Formerly pull and turn knobs arranged individually. Battery now turned 180°, so earth strap shortened to 170 mm. (Formerly 300 mm).
	1132000011	–	Hazard light switch (USA): warning light switched as interior light.
	1332000011	–	Fusebox: modified and bolted above the frame tunnel in the luggage bay (1303). Formerly on the left beside the steering column.
	1332000004 1332000024 (1300 only USA)	–	Brake-indicator-tail light: shape modified (round). Formerly oval.
	1332000011	–	Sealed beam headlight: main beam 60 watt, dipped light 50 watt. Formerly 50 and 40 watt.
11.9.72	1432012747 (141-144)	–	Battery 36 Ah and 45 Ah: now with protective lid.
4.12.72	1132380035	–	Dual-circuit brake warning light: now with 4 lead terminals. Formerly with 5 terminals.

1973

The Beetle is unchanged in appearance this year, though there are some model variations.

VW 1200: The 'Economy Beetle' undergoes its most major modification since 1967. It now has the large round rear lights of the VW 1303 and is fitted with black, silver trimmed bumpers, matching in shape the bumpers of the 1303 Beetle. The decorative grilles are discontinued on the wings. The 1200/34 bhp engine remains unchanged.

VW 1200 L: The L version has as standard equipment chrome finished bumpers, trim strips, and interior trim designed to suppress noise: through-flow ventilation in the rear (without fan); rear shelf; two-speed windscreen wipers with automatic park; reversing lights; driver's sun visor that swivels. Door trim panel on the left with arm rest and pocket. It can be ordered with the 34 or 44 bhp engine.

VW 1303: this Beetle comes in standard 1303 form with a 44 bhp engine. The 1303 L version comes with additional luxury package, the 1303 S with the 50 bhp engine, and the 1303 LS with extra luxury package. The four seater Cabrio is available only in the LS version with 50 bhp.

VW 1303 A: a cheaply priced spin-off of the 'Big Beetle' becomes effectively an additional Economy Beetle. It has similar bodywork, with the more convex windscreen, MacPherson strut front axle and large luggage bay, and also semi-trailing arm rear suspension, but is available in the Federal Republic only with the small 34 bhp engine. Its basic equipment, black bumpers and simple interior fittings correspond to those of the Economy Beetle.

All Beetles with MacPherson strut front suspension are fitted with self-stabilising steering. This enables the vehicle to maintain a straight line in critical driving situations.

Engines above 1300 cc are fitted with an alternator, and have new tensile cylinder heads and longer lasting silencers.

All Beetles including the Karmann Ghia models are fitted with new wheels, which have 41 mm offset.

The Beetles for the US market are equipped with reinforced bumpers, which are fitted additionally with two telescopic shock absorbers. This fulfils the US requirement that they can withstand a collision of at least 8 km/h without sustaining permanent damage.

In January VW brings out the 'Yellow and Black Racer' (Gelbschwarzen Renner) in a special series (3500 vehicles). This Beetle stands out because of its yellow and black paintwork (black engine lid and bonnet). It is based on the VW 1303 S with 50 bhp. Extras: leather sports steering wheel, sport seats, pressed steel wheels size $5^1/_2$ Jx15, 175/70 HR 15 tyres. Price 7650 DM. In September Volkswagen bring out three more special models. The 'Jeans Beetle' 1200/34 bhp: distinctive Tunisian Yellow paintwork. Adhesive stripes on doors and rear hood with the motif 'Jeans'. Denim seat covers with coloured stitching and pockets on the back rests. Black trim mouldings, safety belts, Ludwigshafen radio (MW/VHF). Sports wheels $4^1/_2$ Jx15. Fuel gauge, heated rear window passenger grab-handle, coat hook, anti-dazzle interior mirror, passenger sun visor, 12 volt electrics. Price 5995 DM.

'City Beetle' 1303/44 bhp: special Ibiza Red, Ischia metallic, or Ontario metallic paintwork. Adhesive stripes on doors with motif '1303 City'. Upholstery with broad woven stripes matching colour of body, loop-pile carpet. Inertia-reel seatbelts, radio (SW/MW/LW/VHF), vinyl padded steering wheel. $4^1/_2$ Jx15 sports wheels. Engine hood lock, heated rear window, rubber inserts on bumpers, anti-dazzle interior mirror, reversing lights. Price: 7440 DM. Big-Beetle 1303 S/50 PS: special Hellas metallic paintwork, Ontario metallic or Moon metallic also available. Door decal '1303 Big'. Upholstery in thick cord, loop-pile carpet. Inertia-reel seatbelts, veneered dashboard, vinyl padded steering wheel, styled gearshift knob. $5^{1}/_{2}$ Jx15 sports wheels with steel radial tyres. Engine hood lock, heated rear window, rubber inserts on bumpers, anti-dazzle rear view mirror, reversing lights. Price: 7670 DM.

Dates and facts

1973	Feb.	Representatives of the Nigerian government and of Volkswagen sign on agreement establishing Volkswagen of Nigeria Ltd. In the same year building commences on the factory, 18 km from the Nigerian capital Lagos. Vehicles are to be built here for the Nigerian market.
	May	The medium sized car, the PASSAT is unveiled with a new design concept. (Front-wheel drive, water-cooled 4 cylinder in-line, overhead cam engine, negative roll-radius steering, all-steel monocoque body-work). Engine options: 55, 75 and 85 PS.
	Sept.	The 3,500,000th Transporter since 1950 is built.

VW 1200: Large rear lights with wings modified accordingly. Black painted bumper picked out in silver. As a result of mounting the front bumper higher, the grilles for the horn in the front wing are discontinued. Engine hood lock of plastic.

Special model: the Yellow and Black Racer. Yellow and black paintwork, bonnet and engine lid black. Louvred front apron from US Beetle. Louvres were required in US for air-conditioning system.

The Yellow and Black Racer is based on VW1303 S fitted with 1.6 litre engine.

168

Special model: Big Beetle, 1303S with 50 bhp
engine.

Front axle with stabilising steering roll radius.

Sporty equipment of Yellow and Black Racer:
leather steering wheel, sports seats, 5¹/₂Jx15
wheels, 175/70 HR 15 tyres.

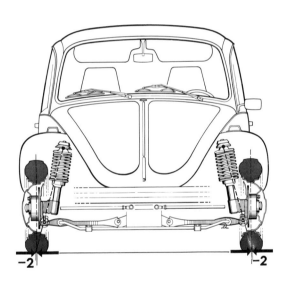

Engine cover with round pressing.

US Beetle: bumpers with telescopic dampers.

169

1973

The most important modifications

Year	Chassis No.	Assembly No.	Modification
Engine/clutch/heating			
29.1.73	1332518621	AD745 528	Distributor: introduction of WB3
1.2.73	1332525131	AB830 938	distributor (USA twin vacuum
	1332525259 (M9)	AB832 668	advance unit discontinued except
	1332526160 (M9)	AD756 892	for California.)
15.3.73	1132674897	AK120 008	
23.3.73	1132690032 (M9)	AH090 024	
1.2.73	1132522922	AD754 870	V-belt pulleys – engine and
	1132523754	AK084 408	generator: galvanised surface.
2.2.73	1132525582 (M9)	AM061 506	Formerly painted black.
6.2.73	1132528475	AB833 834	
7.2.73	1132529803	AH047 206	
10.2.73	1832539493	AG011 796	
23.3.73	1132687765 (M9)	AB870 513	Inlet manifold and exhaust box: new
10.4.73	1132716004	AB884 491	twin preheater tubes. Formerly
2.5.73	1132788570	AC007 869	single tube. Tailpipes changed
			in length and inside diameter.
8.5.73	1132797156	D1085 397	Heat exchangers: heater flap
	1132797411	AK173 444	regulator with springs on floor
	1132800110	AD864 770	vent ducts. Formerly spiral
10.5.73	1132799853	AB902 207	springs on lever mountings.
	1132798706	AH089 047	
11.5.73	1132803570 (M9)	AH096 157	
12.7.73	1132986992	AH101 817	Spark plugs: gap 0.6 mm.
18.7.73	1133018356	D1114 278	Formerly 0.7 mm.
20.7.73	1133021306 (M9)	AH114 026	
1.8.73	1142000003	AS000 001	
31.8.73	1142132421	AS025 502	Timing mark measurement: built-
	1142132876	AR023 056	in top dead centre mark (crankcase
	1342134447 (6 volt)	D1134 996	flywheel).
	1142135046 (12 volt)	D1135 566	
Fuel system			
9.1.73	1132447948	AD749 931	Float for 30 PICT-3
1.2.73	1132524670	D1040 002	carburettor: now expanded foam.
1.3.73	1132606865	AB856 058	Formerly hollow. Air cleaner:
	1132606866	AO789 921	new dry air cleaner with
	1132606867 M157	AK113 791	plastic housing and paper
	1132606868 M240	AC007 758	element. Formerly oil bath air
	1132606869 M240	AF036 654	cleaner.

170

Year	Chassis No.	Assembly No.	Modification
10.5.73	1332802561	–	Fuel tank: full flow filter in fuel line. Formerly strainer in tank. Drain plug discontinued.
1.8.73	1142007917	AR004 158	31 PCIT-4 carburettor: now with replaceable thermostat. Formerly: non-replaceable.
11.9.73	1142147150	AR029 783	31 PICT-4 carburettor: accelerator pump with vent hole. Formerly without.
13.9.73	1142039385 (Emden)	–	Activated carbon container now plastic. Formerly sheet metal.

Front axle/steering

Year	Chassis No.	Assembly No.	Modification
22.1.73	1132509096 (WOB)	–	Jointed steering shaft: lower joint protector discontinued.
12.2.73	1132554359 (Emden)	–	
19.10.73	1142248672	3925 714	Track rod joints: lubrication hole and plugs discontinued.

Rear axle/gears

Year	Chassis No.	Assembly No.	Modification
11.1.73	1132452529	–	Semi-automatic now fitted with parking pawl.

Brakes/wheels/tyres

Year	Chassis No.	Assembly No.	Modification
7.2.73	1132532652	–	Self-adjusting drum brakes (M86): 2 spring retainers on secondary shoe. Formerly 1 spring retainer.
7.2.73	1132529939	–	Tandem brake master cylinder: single brake light switch. Formerly: two.

Bodywork

Year	Chassis No.	Assembly No.	Modification
28.2.73	1332623529	–	Fresh air control VW 1303: fixed by hollow screw direct to switch panel. Formerly: fixed by hex screws to securing flanges of switch panel.
5.3.73	1532541768	–	Rear window: window moved 30 mm upwards.
1.8.73	1142000001 (111/112) (115/116)	– –	Paintwork: new: Atlas White, Senegal Red, Sahara Beige. Continued lines: Marina Blue, Bright Orange. Discontinued: Pastel White, Texas yellow.
	(113/114, 133) (135/136)	– –	New: Atlas White, Senegal Red. Sahara Beige, Marina Blue, Tropic Green, Rally Yellow, Cliff Green, Metallic Hellas, Metallic Moss. Continued lines: Metallic Marathon, Metallic Alaska. Discontinued: Biscay Blue, Sumatra Green, Metallic Turquoise.

Year	Chassis No.	Assembly No.	Modification
	(141-144) (151/152)	–	Continued lines: Light Ivory, Bahia Red, Saturn Yellow, Olympia Blue, Phoenix Red, Sun Yellow, Zambezi Green, Ravenna Green, Metallic Saturn Yellow, Metallic Alaska, Metallic Marathon.
1.8.73	1342000005 (1303) (15)	–	Ventilation: fresh and warm air outlet jets to right and left below windscreen. Formerly full width ventilation. Glove box cover: push button lock. Formerly rotary lock.
	(USA only)		Front and rear bumpers: new: reinforced bumpers incorporating shock absorbers.
	1142000001 (Excluding Type 181)	–	Three point safety belt (home models only): now fitted as standard, with lap-strap.
	1142000001	–	Body sill panels strengthened in jacking point area.
24.9.73	1142165704	–	Three point seat: detent for forward-folded backrest discontinued.
1.12.73	1142357000	–	Inertia reel seatbelt: guide for belt strap.

Electrics

Year	Chassis No.	Assembly No.	Modification
4.1.73 1.8.73	1332445273 (USA) 1142000001	– –	Generator: new alternator with voltage regulator. Formerly DC generator with control box.
24.9.73	1142153057	–	Headlights: reflector and lens bonded. Formerly separate.
4.4.73	1132706420	–	Brake-light switch: switch in second brake circuit discontinued.
20.11.73	1442289990 1442290456 1442284248 1442287868	D1180 130 AR066 102 AH233 684 AH177 920 (M9)	Generator V-belt pulley: new: rear half without locating slot in hub. Formerly with locating tab. Round hole in hub.
22.11.73	1342343700	AS085 132	

1974

The Beetle range is cut down and simultaneously an identifying feature for this year's models is introduced: the front indicators on all Beetle models are incorporated into the bumpers, ribs are moulded into the number plate lights.

To accommodate the catalytic converter for the US version, the rear valance over the engine is curved in profile. The silencer pipes are black (formerly chrome plated).

The US versions are fitted with a fuel-injected engine, exhaust pump and catalytic converter to run on lead-free petrol. The exhaust box on these models has only one tailpipe. The front indicators are still mounted on the wings.

VW1200 equipment is more spartan for reasons of cost. The hub caps are done away with and replaced by plastic caps covering the wheel centres and nuts. The glove box lid is discontinued, instead the aperture is fitted with a plastic surround. The driver's sun visor and door- and side-panelling undergo small changes.

For those wanting a better equipped Economy Beetle, the 'L' package is available. It includes extra sound insulation, window trims and a lockable glove compartment. Also, chrome plated bumpers, padded dashboard and through flow ventilation, though without additional air inlets in the bonnet lid and dashboard.

To reduce the amount of effort required to operate the clutch pedal, the clutch cable is re-routed. An electronic voltage regulator replaces the previous mechanical one.

The 1200 model is available with optional 34 or 44 bhp engine.

All Beetles with long front-end are in future to be designated 1303. All 'L' and 'S' suffixes are removed from the badging on the tail of the car. Because of the new rack and pinion steering, the steering damper is discontinued on these models.

Engine options on the 1303 are 34, 44 or 50 bhp, 'L' equipment may also be chosen. The four-seater Cabrio is only available with the 1.6 litre, 50 bhp engine.

The production of the Karmann Ghia is halted. In the period 1955–1974 362,000 Coupés were built. The Ghia Cabrio appeared in 1957. A total of 81,000 of this model were built. From March Karmann builds the Scirocco instead of the Ghia.

1974 Feb./ March   The Scirocco, the new two-door, four-seater coupé with large hatchback goes on display. This newcomer with the transverse engine is to be built by Karmann. Three engine types are offered: 50, 75 and 85 bhp.

May   The Golf – the small VW – has its Press launch. After the Passat and Scirocco, the Golf is the third model of the new product generation. It is produced in both two- and four-door hatchback form. There is a choice of 50 bhp and 70 bhp engines, the latter running on standard petrol.

1.7.   At 19 minutes past eleven the last Beetle from the parent factory at Wolfsburg comes off the line. Since 1945, 11,916,519 of these cars have been built. Now the vehicle is produced exclusively in the Hanover, Emden and Brussels factories. The line switches to production of the Golf, and later the Audi

50. Beetle bodyshells and other parts continue to be made at Wolfsburg.

July   The six-year production run of the VW 412 comes to an end; the VW K70 continues with two engine options, 75 and 100 bhp. Since 1959 VW do Brasil has built 1.5 million Beetles.

Sept.   Launch of the Audi 50, newest of the VW group's models. The 5-seater small car, overall only 3.49m in length, comes in two versions: Audi 50 LS with 50 bhp engine and Audi 50 GL with 60 bhp engine.

4.10.   The 18 millionth Beetle comes off the Emden line. In motoring history, no other car has been produced for so long or in such numbers. Worldwide, a further 2600 cars are built every day.

6.11.   Hans Birnbaum, chairman of the board of Salzgitter AG, is elected chairman of the supervisory committed.

Curved rear valance. Exhaust tailpipes black, formerly chrome plated.

Front indicators incorporated into bumper.

VW 1200: Hub caps dicontinued. Plastic caps fitted instead over wheel centres and wheel nuts.

For US and Japanese markets: 1.6 litre 50 bhp engine with fuel-injection equipment.

1974   The most important modifications

Year	Chassis No.		Assembly No.	Modification
Engine/clutch/heating				
11.2.74	1842541476		AL005 039 AM011 798	Engine for general purpose vehicle: now with heat exchangers as Type 1. Formerly without.
12.6.74	1142802587		D1271 798	Distributor, 34 bhp engine: new combined centrifugal and vacuum advance/retard. Formerly vacuum advance/retard only.
Front axle/steering				
29.1.74	1142487143		–	Stabilizer bar mounting to underside of frame: captive nuts welded on. Formerly threaded sockets.
1.8.74	1352000001		–	Steering: rack and pinion steering. Formerly worm and roller steering.
Rear axle/gears				
12.12.74	1152142154		–	Bearing cap for torsion bar (swing axle): bearing cap stamped with ribs.
Bodywork				
19.2.74	1142509962		–	Steel sunroof, rear drain tube: tube terminates at side of engine compartment. Formerly tube terminated in rear side panel above running board.
11.4.74	1142683124		–	Front seat backrest: new backrest similar to Passat.
1.8.74	1152000001	not USA Canada or Japan	–	Front bumper: bumper altered to take indicators.
		not 1200 or 1200L	–	Front and rear bumpers: bumper carriers strengthened with slot for tow-rope. Formerly towing eyes. Rear valance curved, ribbed number plate light.
1.8.74	1152000001		111,112 115,116	VW 1200: new: Ceylon Beige, Marino Yellow, Miami Blue, Lofoten Green. Continued lines: Senegal Red, Atlas White. Discontinued: Sahara Beige, Marina Blue, Brilliant Orange.
1.8.74	1152000001		113/114 133 135/136	VW 1200L & VW 1303: new: Black Ceylon Beige, Marino Yellow, Phoenix Red, Miami Blue, Lofoten Green, Metallic Ancona, Metallic Viper Green. Continued lines: Atlas White, Senegal Red, Rally Yellow, Cliff Green, Metallic Green, Metallic Marathon. Discontinued: Sahara Beige.

176

Year	Chassis No.	Assembly No.	Modification
			Marina Blue, Tropic Green, Metallic Moss, Metallic Alaska.
		151/152	New: Black, Berber Yellow, Nepal Orange, Ibiza Red, Malaga Red, Lagoon Blue, Metallic Ancona, Metallic Palma, Metallic Diamond Silver. Continued lines: Light Ivory, Sun Yellow.

Electrics

Year	Chassis No.	Assembly No.	Modification
21.1.74	1142458359	–	Oil pressure switch: now with shroud.
1.2.74	1142489588	–	Intermittent wipe relay now with simultaneous wash/wipe.

1975

The Beetle reverts to its old design and old suspension, trailing arm at the front and swing-axle at the rear. The long front end configuration (1303) is now produced only for the Cabrio. The Economy Beetle is the only survivor of the range with two engine options, namely the familiar 1200/34 bhp and the 1600/50 bhp with 12 volt electrics. An 'M' package, comprising fuel gauge, anti-dazzle mirror, passenger grab-handle and heated rear window is offered. 'L' equipment includes chrome plated bumpers with rubber strips, chrome hub caps, reversing lights, fresh air system with fan and through-flow ventilation ('ears' in rear side panels).

The VW 1200L 50 bhp comes equipped with compensating spring on rear axle and front disc brakes. This model also has the louvred engine cover as fitted to the 1303 model.

After production of the VW 1303 ends, the custom model for the US market is upgraded with equipment comparable to the European 1200 L: chrome window surrounds, improved sound insulation, two-speed fan, heated rear window. Mechanically, the vehicle remains unchanged: fuel-injection, exhaust pump, catalytic converter, double-joint rear axle and drum brakes all round.

Dates and facts

1975	10. 1.	Rudolf Leiding resigns from chairmanship of VW AG.
	10. 2.	Toni Schmücker, formerly a member of the supervisory committee, takes over as chairman of VW AG.
	March	The Polo is launched. The two-door small saloon with large hatchback is powered by a 900 cc water-cooled transverse engine developing 40 bhp. Mechanically, and in terms of bodywork, the Polo is similar to the Audi 50.
		In Lagos, the new VW factory of Volkswagen Nigeria Ltd comes on stream. A workforce of 1,100 will build about 60 vehicles per day. The factory is a joint venture between VW AG and the Nigerian Government.
		The 500,000th vehicle is built in Mexico. 11,000 workers produce 550 cars every day in the factory in Puebla.
	April	Alongside the long-serving VW Transporter there is now a new commercial vehicle, the 'LT'. It is a modern freight carrying vehicle in three weight classes from 1.25 - 1.75 tonnes. The new LT range is to be built in the Hanover factory.
	July	New warranty terms for all VW and Audi-NSU models: from July 9th there is a worldwide unlimited mileage guarantee of one year. The guarantee on the new LT is limited to 50,000 kilometres.
	Sept.	At the IAA Frankfurt (Frankfurt Motor Show) the Golt GTi is unveiled. The GTi (0-100 km/h in 9 seconds) has a top speed of 182 km/h. The four cylinder in-line engine with mechanical fuel-injection (K-Jetronic) develops 110 bhp from its 1.6 litres.

Beetle saloon (VW 1200) now only available with short front end. The wing beading, formerly the same colour as the bodywork, now only comes in black.

VW 1200: in addition to through flow ventilation, a feature of Beetle 'L's since 1973, 'L' equipment now includes a two-speed electric ventilation fan.

1975   The most important modifications

Year	Chassis No.	Assembly No.	Modification
Engine/clutch/heating			
1.8.75	1162000001	–	Air cleaner, 1.2 litre engine: dry air cleaner with plastic housing and paper element. Formerly oil bath air cleaner. New thermostatically controlled inlet air preheating.
Bodywork			
1.8.75	1162000001	VW 1200	Paintwork: new: Black, Ocean Blue. Continued lines: Marino Yellow, Lofoten Green, Senegal Red, Atlas White. Discontinued: Ceylon Beige, Miami Blue.
		VW 1200L	New: Ocean Blue, Metallic Topaz, Metallic Diamond Silver. Continued lines: Black, Rally Yellow, Marino Yellow, Phoenix Red, Senegal Red, Lofoten Green, Atlas White, Metallic Viper Green.
		VW 1303 Cabrio	Continued lines: Black, Sun Yellow, Light Ivory, Nepal Orange, Ibiza Red, Malaga Red, Lagoon Blue, Metallic Ancona, Metalic Viper Green, Metallic Diamond Silver. Discontinued: Berber Yellow, Metallic Palma.
1.8.75		–	Number plate light: now of plastic, top surface ribbed.
Electrics			
16.1.75	1152160733	–	Screen washer: washer bottle fitted with strainer.
26.2.75	1152174666	AF129 026 AR132 638	Suppressed generator (M613): now alternator. Formerly DC generator.
14.10.75	1162043569	AC008 644 AS270 694	
1.8.75	1162000001	–	VW 1200 electrics: now 12 volt. Formerly 6 volt.
General modifications			
31.7.75	1152266092	–	Volkswagen Type 1303 production ceases.
31.7.75	1152266092	–	Volkswagen Type 1: 1.3 litre 44 bhp engine discontinued.

1976

The Beetle, apart from the new colour range, remains unaltered.

1976	June	There is now also a GTi version of the Scirocco powered by the 110 bhp engine. Acceleration 0-100 km/h in 8.8 sec. Top speed 185 km/h.
	Sept.	The Golf with 50 bhp diesel engine is unveiled.
	October	The millionth Golf rolls off the Wolfsburg line.
		After lengthy consideration and negotiation the VW company decides to establish an assembly plant in the USA. Westmoreland, Pennsylvania is chosen as the location. The aim is a yearly output of 200,000 Golfs by 1979 from 4,000 workers.
		The Volkswagen and Audi-NSU sales organisation at home is restructured. Instead of the previous 80 Volkswagen main dealers and 7 Audi-NSU distribution centres, there are to be 22 distribution centres supplying the 3,400 dealers and service outlets with vehicles, spares and accessories.
	26.11.	The 30 millionth Volkswagen is built.

1976   **The most important modifications**

Year	Chassis No.	Assembly No.	Modification
Bodywork			
1.8.76	1172000001	VW 1200 1100, 1120	Paintwork: new: Riadh Yellow, Panama Brown, Mars Red, Miami Blue, Manila Green, Bali Green, Polar White. Continued line: Black. Discontinued: Ocean Blue, Marino Yellow, Lofoten Green, Senagal Red, Atlas White.
		VW 1200L 1111, 1121	New: Riadh Yellow, Dakota Beige, Panama Brown, Mars Red, Brocade Red, Miami Blue, Manila Green, Bali Green, Polar White, Metallic Timor Brown, Metallic Bronze, Metallic Bahama Blue. Continued lines: Black, Metallic Viper Green, Metallic Diamond Silver. Discontinued: Ocean Blue, Metallic Topaz, Rally Yellow, Marino Yellow, Phoenix Red, Senegal Red, Lofoten Green, Atlas White.
		VW 1303 Cabrio 1511, 1521	New: Marino Yellow, Mars Red Reef Blue, Polar White, Metallic Brazil Brown, Metallic Black. Continued lines: Black, Malaga Red, Metallic Ancona, Metallic Viper Green, Metallic Diamond Silver

1977

The Economy Beetle remains unaltered. It is available with optional 'L' equipment and either the 34 or 50 bhp engine.

1977	March	With the new generation of Volkswagens, the company has managed to develop a range to suit the wishes of almost every customer, and all within the space of only four years. The Derby, the last in this new line of products, is shown to the public for the first time in spring. It was developed from the Polo and is intended to appeal to purchasers of conservative taste.
	May	Volkswagen provides the German State Railway's largest single customer account. Incoming materials for production processes, as well as finished vehicles, are for the most part carried by rail. On 16 May the 100,000th train leaves the Wolfsburg factory.

The most important modifications

Year	Chassis No.	Assembly No.	Modification
Bodywork			
1.8.77	1182000001	VW 1200L	Paintwork: new: Alpine White, Malaga Red. Continued lines: Riadh Yellow, Dakota Beige, Panama Brown, Mars Red, Miami Blue, Manila Green, Bali Green, Metallic Kolibri Green. Discontinued: Brocade Red, Polar White, Metallic Timor Brown, Metallic Bronze, Metallic Bahama Blue, Metallic Viper Green, Metallic Diamond Silver, Black.
		VW 1303 Cabrio	New: Alpine White, Metallic Kolibri Green. Continued lines: Black, Marino Yellow, Mars Red, Malaga Red, Blue, Metallic Brazil Brown, Metallic Ancona, Metallic Viper Green, Metallic Diamond Silver. Discontinued: Polar White, Brocade Red, Agate Brown, Metallic Timor Brown, Metallic Bronze, Metallic Bahama Blue.

1978

This year, there are no modifications to what remains of the Beetle range (50 bhp engine no longer available). At the beginning of the year German production of the Beetle (at Emden) ceases. The VW 1200L is imported into Germany from Mexico with 34 bhp engine, radial tyres, side trim, fuel gauge, heated rear window, anti-dazzle mirror, passenger grab-handle, inertia reel seatbelts and adjustable head restraints. The two-speed electric ventilation fan is no longer fitted. The AC generator is replaced by a DC generator.

Beetles from Mexico have a smaller rear window (879 x 408 mm) which was fitted on German versions between 1965 and 1971. From August 1965 until the end of 1977 the rear window measured 879 x 446 mm.

The rear valance above the silencer is once again flat, as it was on German-produced vehicles until August 1974. The headlining extends to below the rear window.

The silencer tailpipes, like the running-board trim, are once more chrome plated. The Mexican Beetle has louvres in the engine cover (until July 81) which had been a feature of the 50 bhp Beetle. Price: 8145 DM, Cabrio 13845 DM.

Dates and facts

1978	19.1.	The Beetle is no longer produced in Europe. The car is now shipped from Mexico to satisfy continuing demand for it.
		Much public interest surrounds the delivery of 10,000 Golfs to the GDR.
	May	The 125,000th Volkswagen built for the Federal Post Office is handed over to the Minister, Herr Gscheidle, in Bonn.
	4.7.	The annual general meeting of Volkswagenwerk AG votes to increase the share capital by 300 million DM to 1200 million DM. This is effected in the first half of September and represents the largest single increase in share capital in the history of the Federal Republic's Stock Exchange.
	31.7.	The Volkswagen Manufacturing Corporation of America, founded in 1976, merges with the former distribution company Volkswagen of America to become Volkswagen of America, Inc, based in Warren, Michigan.
	August	Introduction of the Passat Diesel. VW's own diesel engine, a six-cylinder, is fitted to the LT. The 'LT 40' and 'LT 45' are additions to the range.
	20.11.	Introduction of Volkswagen shares on the Vienna Stock Exchange.
	Nov.	The 'Iltis', an all-purpose vehicle with 4-wheel drive is produced in Ingolstadt from November onwards.

The most important modifications

Year	Chassis No.	Assembly No.	Modification
1.8.78	1192000001	VW 1200	Paintwork: new: Mexico Beige, Florida Blue. Continued lines: Mars Red, Manila Green, Alpine White. Discontinued: Black, Riadh Yellow, Dakota Beige, Panama Brown Miami Blue, Bali Green, Metallic Bronze, Metallic Bahama Blue, Metallic Viper Green, Metallic Diamond Silver, Metallic Kolibri Green.
		VW Cabrio	New: Lemon Yellow, Florida Blue, Metallic Indiana Red, Metallic Platinum, Metallic River Blue, Metallic Pearl. Continued lines: Black, Mars Red, Alpine White, Metallic Brazil Brown, Metallic Kolibri Green, Metallic Diamond Silver. Discontinued: Marino Yellow, Malaga Red, Reef Blue, Metallic Ancona, Metallic Viper Green.

The VW Beetle from Mexico; from January onwards available only in 'L' form. 'L' specification, however, no longer includes the two-speed electric ventilation fan.

In January 1978 the last Beetle constructed in Germany comes off the Emden line. The Cabrio continues to be built by Karmann.

Headlining extended to below rear window.

Silencer tailpipes and trim on running-board are chrome plated. Louvred engine cover. Rear valance is once again flat.

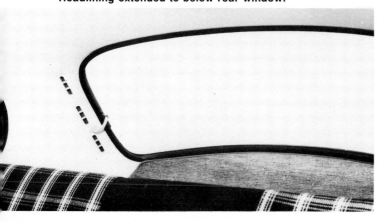

1979

Apart from the new colour range, there are no modifications.

Year	Chassis No.	Assembly No.	Modification
Bodywork			
1.8.79	11A0000001	VW 1200	Paintwork: continued lines: Lido Green. Special edition 'Silver Bug': Metallic Diamond Silver. Discontinued: Florida Blue.
		VW Cabrio	Continued lines: Lemon Yellow, Mars Red, Florida Blue, Alpine White, Metallic River Blue, Metallic Diamond Silver, Black.

1980

After a production run of 332,000 over 31 years the production of the Beetle Cabrio, the most prolific open car in the world, ceases on 10 January 1980. The very last Beetle Cabriolet to be built, chassis No. 152044140, forms part of the Karmann Motor Collection in Osnabrück.
VW 1200L (34 bhp): Florida Blue no longer available, otherwise no modifications.

Production of the Beetle Cabrio ceases on 10 January.

Dashboard of 'L' specification Mexican Beetle. The steering wheel is still adorned with the Wolfsburg crest. The wheel is finished in grain-effect plastic.

1981

On Friday 15 May 1981, the 20 millionth Beetle rolls off the Puebla line. To mark this unique occasion, the special edition 'Silver Bug' is available.

The Silver Bug with 1.2 litre engine (34 bhp) is a sparkling sight: metallic silver paintwork, black stripes and, on the tail, a reference to the '20 million' landmark. The interior is trimmed with black and white tartan fabric upholstery with matching door and side trim. Along with this equipment there are also a radio with VHF and MW bands, heated rear window and radial tyres.

Some Beetles have a screen-washer bottle with integral electric pump instead of the pneumatic type.

The shift lever carries the commemorative plaque. This special model costs 9,380 DM.

On 30 July 1981 the louvred engine cover is discontinued, and from chassis No. 113020000 onwards, the Beetle is only available fitted with a laminated windscreen. At the same time the dual-circuit brake warning light is incorporated into the speedometer.

The brake warning light is situated next to the speedometer.

Dates and facts

1981	5.3.	100 methanol-fuelled Volkswagens are authorised for use in a test programme in Berlin.
	8.3.	25th anniversary of the Hanover VW Factory.
	March	At the Geneva Motor Show the new Scirocco is launched.
		Volkswagen Caminhoes Ltda of Brazil commences production of the medium 11-13 tonne truck.
		Production of the Diesel Transporter at the Hanover factory.
	20.3.	The 5 millionth exchange engine is built at the Kassel works.
	April	A contract is signed for assembly of Beetles in Egypt.
		Workers at the Westmoreland factory turn out VW of America's 500,000th Rabbit.
	15.5.	Production record: the 20 millionth VW beetle.
	23.6.	Karmann in Osnabrück coachbuild their 1,500,000th Volkswagen.
	26.8.	The 5,000th VW-MAN truck leaves the Hannover factory.
	Sept.	Announcement of agreement on a collaboration contract between VW AG and the Nissan motor Co Ltd of Tokyo.
	Oct.	Decision to build a Canadian component factory at Barrie, Ontario to supply the US market.
	13.11.	Dr Carl H.Hahn is nominated as new boss of VW to succeed Toni Schmücker.
	14.12.	The first VW Transporter produced by the workforce of Volkswagen Argentina SA, Buenos Aires rolls off the line.

In Puebla, Mexico on 15 May 1981 the 20 millionth Beetle rolls off the production line.

Special edition 'Silver Bug' to commemorate the Beetle's run of 20 million vehicles.

Silver Bug: keyring

Silver Bug: commemorative plaque on gear shift lever.

From 31 July 1981 the engine cover is no longer louvred.

Silver Bug: wheel trim.

Brake warning light to right of speedometer.

Screenwasher bottle with integral electric washer pump.

1981   The most important modifications

Year	Chassis No.	Assembly No.	Modification
Bodywork			
1981	11C 000001	–	Colours as 1980 range: Mexico Beige, Mars Red, Lido Green, Alpine White.
1982			

1982

From the middle of May the Beetle is officially fitted with an electric screenwasher pump. Also, the dual-circuit brake warning light, whose function was to warn of failure of one of the brake circuits, is replaced by a brake fluid level gauge.

In spring 1982 the special edition 'Jeans Bug' goes on sale, available in either Alpine White or Mars Red. Special equipment comprises the following items: stripes on lower door and side panels with 'Jeans Bug' motif, similar motif on engine cover. Front and rear bumpers are picked out with silver stripes. Following parts finished in black: exhaust tailpipes, window frames, trim strips, headlamp trim, boot, bonnet and door locks, trims and running boards, hubcaps, aerial and exterior mirror. Interior equipment includes 'Salzgitter' radio, denim upholstery with pockets on front seats, door and side trim panels in blue vinyl. Jetta gearshift knob with inlaid 'Jeans' motif. Head restraints are denim faced. A leather 'jeans' patch is sewn on to the side of the seatbacks. The Jeans Bug is powered by the familiar 1.2 litre 34 bhp engine and costs 9,995 DM.

A further special model follows in September of the same year: the 'Special Bug' comes in Mars Red or Metallic Black. The following equipment is finished in black: silencer tailpipes, front and rear bumpers with gold stripes, window trims and trim strips, rear lamp cluster mountings, headlamp trims, boot, bonnet and door locks, running board cover, wheel trims, hubcaps, aerial and exterior mirror. Above the lower edge of the door and below the side-trim strips are god stripes. The 'Special Bug' motif on engine cover and boot lid are also gold. Interior equipment includes 'Salzgitter' radio, leather/fabric upholstery with seat facings in black and gold tartan. The Jetta gearshift knob is fitted, inlaid with the 'Special Bug' motif. Head re-straints are covered in black cloth. Price for the Special Bug fitted with 34 bhp engine: 10,045 DM. Colours available: Velvet Orange, Mars Red, Selvas Green, Alpine White.

Dates and facts

1982	4.1.	Dr Carl H.Hahn takes over as chairman of the board of Volks-wagenwerk AG.
	25.2.	The 5 millionth Golf is completed at the Wolfsburg plant.
	8.6.	A trial assembly contract is agreed with the Shanghai Trac-tor and Automobile Corpor-ation; this forms the basic agreement for a joint venture with the Shanghai Tractor and Automobile Corporation and the Shanghai Branch of the Bank of China, reached on November 29th. The aim is to assemble the Volkswagen Santana in the People's Re-public of China.
	30.9.	Agreement is reached with the Spanish motor manufacturer SEAT (Sociedad Espanola de Automoviles de Turismo SA) detailing collaboration, licens-ing and technical support.
	8.11.	The 20 millionth vehicle to be produced at the Wolfsburg works, a Golf Turbo Diesel, rolls off the line.

On the jeans Bug, window trims, door-handles, bumpers, headlamp trims and exterior mirrors are finished in black.

Motif on rear sidepanel of Jeans Bug.

Black and red Jeans Bug' motif on engine cover.

The leather Jeans patch on the denim upholstered seats.

1983

Production of the Beetle continues with no technical modifications, though a number of special models are produced this year.

In spring the 'Aubergine Beetle' with 1.2 litre engine goes on sale. Paintwork is Metallic Aubergine with matching wheels and chrome plated wheel trims. Silver stripes adorn its sides.

Upholstery is in an aubergine shade with co-ordinated vinyl. Door and side panelling appears in the same colour. Chrome plated bumpers round off the Aubergine Beetle which comes with a 'Braunschweig' radio as standard.

3,300 Aubergine Beetles are sold in West Germany in 1983. Price: 9480 DM.

Along with the Aubergine Beetle a Metallic Ice Blue Beetle is also offered during 1983, sales total 2000 in this year.

This Beetle, costing 9,760 DM, has black and silver stripes above the lower edge of the door and chrome plated wheel trims.

The upholstery, including head restraints is in blue-grey cloth, while the luggage space behind the rear seats is lined in grey-blue. This special Beetle is also equipped with a 'Braunschweig' radio.

The special Apline White model has chrome plated wheel trims and black and silver body stripes. Upholstery is in blue-grey cloth; the 'Braunschweig' radio is only fitted as an optional extra.

Standard Beetles are available in Mars Red, Apline White, Atlantic Blue, Velvet Orange (until July 83), Selvas Green. Cloth trim: black and white.

Dates and facts

1983	11.4.	The first Santana assembled in China is completed.
		To meet the many demands involved in intensive research into automobile manufacture, and to contribute to the future security of the enterprise, a new research centre is brought into operation. It consists of 9,000 sq m of offices and laboratories plus 6,000 sq m of workshops and test facilities.
	June	Production of the new Golf, replacing the first generation Golf after its nine-year production life, commences at the same time as the new final assembly shop 54 comes into service. In this new building the most modern technology is employed combining improved productivity with more satisfactory working conditions.
	22.12.	The 100,000th new Golf is produced.

Aubergine Beetle with double side stripes and chrome plated wheel trims.

Metallic Ice Blue Beetle with black and white side stripes, chrome plated wheel trims, and fabric upholstery and luggage compartment lining in blue-grey Panama tweed.

1984

In February of this year there is a new version of the special Metallic Ice Blue model, costing 9,990 DM. In 1984 a total of 1,800 examples of this model were sold.

In the same month the 'Sunny Bug' goes on sale at a price of 9,990 DM. A total of 1,800 Sunny Bugs are available.

The Sun Yellow Sunny Bug has a black and white side stripe and a similar stripe below the side trim strip. Chrome plated wheel trims are also standard. The cord ribbed upholstery is a curry shade. Like all Beetle models since 1978, the Sunny Bug is powered by the 1.2 litre 34 bhp engine.

The 'Velvet Red Beetle' is introduced in mid-1984 and in November the price of the 1200 beetle exceeds the 10,000 DM mark by a considerable amount. The Velvet Red Beetle costing 10,525 DM (price in July 9,990 DM, in September 10,175 DM) has blue stripes below the side trim strips and similar stripes on the lower part of the body. In addition, flowers adorn the sides of the car. The Velvet Red Beetle also has chrome plated wheel trims but the 'Braunschweig' radio is an optional extra.

The upholstery is in red and blue striped velour and Mauritius blue vinyl. Door and side-trim on the interior are also in blue vinyl. Despite the hefty price increase, 2,600 Velvet Red Beetles are sold in 1984.

Only the brake drums are altered on the standard Beetle. From chassis No. 11 E 011590 onwards they have a strengthened outer ring.

The standard Beetle costs 10,525 DM from 5.11.84 and is supplied in Mars Red, Atlantic Blue, Selvas Green and Alpine White.

Dates and facts

1984   January   The new Volkswagen Jetta is launched. Volkswagen present the IRVW III, based on the new Jetta. Along with high performance, together with better active safety, this design study also seeks optimum comfort; at the same time, the safety standards and exhaust emission levels required by law are also fulfilled. The power unit is a 180 bhp water-cooled supercharged in-line engine.

1985 and on

After 50 years and more than 20 million units the Beetle era is coming to an end – for Germany, at least – with a jubilee model. This is a Beetle in tin grey metallic finish with tinted green windows and a silver-coloured badge. On the 20 August 1985 the last consignment of Beetles, from Mexico, arrive in Germany.

What was achieved with the Beetle, what surrounded it, is so unique that it will not be repeated. This model has actively helped to shape fifty years of the one hundred year history of the automobile. In its best years far in excess of one million units were produced annually. To date 20.6 million Beetles have been assembled in twenty countries. It was Germany's best ambassador and it was represented in practically every country of the world. The list of 151 export countries reaches from Angola to the Soviet Union. Alone in the USA more than 400,000 Beetles were sold annually at the height of its success.

But even now the Beetle is not dead, for it is still built on the Mexican production line. Rumour has it that the line is to close in only a few years – but rumour has tried to kill-off the Beetle many times before . . .

Last of the line? The Beetle Jubilee model, with boot badge shown above.

Interior of the Jubilee Beetle.

Beetle type and model designations

Model designations 1949

Type
11	Standard Saloon
11A	Export Saloon

Model designations 1954

VW 1200				
Type A	Type B	Designation	Series	Official Type Desig.
111	112	Standard Saloon	1.2 l	11
113	114	Export Saloon	1.2 l	11
115	116	Standard Saloon with sun roof	1.2 l	11
117	118	Export Saloon with sun roof	1.2 l	11
141	–	Cabriolet, 2-seater (Hebmüller)		14
151	152	Cabriolet, 4-seater (Karmann)	1.2 l	15

A = left-hand drive; B = right-hand drive

Model designations August 1963

VW 1200			
LH Drive	RH Drive	Designation	Official Type Desig.
111	112	Saloon*	
113	114	Saloon, Export	
115	116	Saloon, with sliding roof	11
117	118	Saloon, Export, with steel wind-back roof	
141	142	Karmann Ghia Cabriolet, 2-seater	
143	144	Karmann Ghia Coupé	14
151	152	Cabriolet, 4-seater	15

* With 30 PS engine, previously Standard Model

197

Model designations August 1967

		VW 1200 1300 and 1500			
Type A	Type B	Designation	Series	Equipment Extras, special	Official Type Desig.
111 115	112 116	VW 1200 VW 1200 with steel wind-back roof	1.2 l	–	
113 117	114 118	VW 1300 VW 1300 with steel wind-back roof	1.3 l	M 88: 1.2 l	11
113	114	VW 1500	1.5 l	M 157: 1.5 l with emission control syst.	
141 143	142 144	VW 1500 Karmann Ghia Cabriolet VW 1500 Karmann Ghia Coupé	1.5 l	M 157: 1.5 l	14
147	–	VW delivery van	1.2 l	–	147
151	152	VW 1500 Cabriolet	1.5 l	M 157: 1.5 l with emission control syst.	15

A = l/hand drive; B = r/hand drive; M 157: USA only

Model designations 1968

Since August 1968 Beetle models and versions have been registered with a 6-figure identification number.

The significance of these figures is as follows:

1st figure = Type
2nd figure = Model
3rd figure – Version (or finish, style)
4th figure – Index
5th figure – Engine no.
6th figure – Transmission no.

Engine identification numbers:

1 = 1200 cc
2 = 1300 cc
3 = 1500 cc
4 = 1500 with emission control system (M 157)

Transmission identification nos:

1 = 4-speed manual geabox
2 = semi-automatic

Model designations for this year:

11 = VW 1200/VW 1300/1500
14 = VW 1500 Karmann Ghia Cabriolet/Coupé
147 – VW delivery van
15 = VW 1500 Cabriolet

Model designations 1972

The very varied models and versions of the
VW Beetle Type 1 were indicated by a 6-figure
identification number.
Example: 135 131 indicates Type 1, 1303 Sa-
loon, left-hand drive, L version, 1600 cc, 50
PS (37 kW), 4-speed manual gearbox

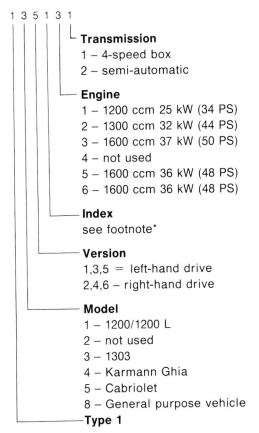

1 3 5 1 3 1

Transmission
1 – 4-speed box
2 – semi-automatic

Engine
1 – 1200 ccm 25 kW (34 PS)
2 – 1300 ccm 32 kW (44 PS)
3 – 1600 ccm 37 kW (50 PS)
4 – not used
5 – 1600 ccm 36 kW (48 PS)
6 – 1600 ccm 36 kW (48 PS)

Index
see footnote*

Version
1,3,5 = left-hand drive
2,4,6 – right-hand drive

Model
1 – 1200/1200 L
2 – not used
3 – 1303
4 – Karmann Ghia
5 – Cabriolet
8 – General purpose vehicle

Type 1

Figs 1 – 6 refer to places in the identification no.

Designation	**Types, 1 – 3 l/hand drive	r/hand	Index 4	Engine 5	Trans- mission 6
Saloon 1200/1200 L	111	112	0 – 1	1 – 2 – 3	1 – 2
Saloon 1200 North America	113	–	7 – 8	6	1 – 2
Saloon 1303/1303 A	135	136	0	1 – 2 – 3	1 – 2
Saloon 1303 North America	133	–	0	1 – 2 – 3	1 – 2
Cabriolet (4-seater)	151	152	1	2 – 3	1 – 2
Cabriolet (4-seater) North America	153	–	0	6	1 – 2
General purpose vehicle	181	182	0 – 1	5 – 6	1

* Index 1 = L version; 7 – 8 = custom model for North America

Key to chassis numbers

Saloon chassis were numbered in series from 1940. From 20 December 1941 a figure 1 was placed before the chassis number, indicating the Type 1 (Beetle).

From 1 August 1964 a 9-digit chassis number (115 000 001) was used, which was extended to 10 digits on 1 August 1969. The chassis number breaks down as follows: the first digit stands for Type 1 (VW Beetle); the second for the model. Thus 14 = the Karmann Ghia based on the Type 1; 13 = the VW 1303. The third digit represents the model year (this changes every 1 August). Thus from 1 August 1965 the number 146 510 150 would break down as 14 = Karmann Ghia based on the Type 1; 6 = model year 1966. After these first three digits comes the serial production number, starting at 000 001 for each model year.

Since 1980 there has been a standardised international chassis number applying to all vehicle manufacturers. The explanation of the 17 letters and digits is as follows:

1	2	3	4	5	6	7	8	9	10	11	12	13	14	15	16	17
W	V	W	Z	Z	Z	1	1	Z	B	M	1	2	3	4	5	6

Position	Explanation
1 – 3	**Manufacturers' code:** WVW = VW AG/(private) car types WV2 = VW AG/Transporter (Type 2 and LT) WAU = Audi 1WV = Volkswagen of America, private car models 1V1 = Volkswagen of America, pick-up models
4 – 6	Fill-in letters (three Zs, except USA and Canada)
7, 8	2-digit abbreviated designation of type, from the first two figures of the official type designation
9	Further fill-in letters (also a Z, except for USA and Canada)
10	Indicates year of manufacture/model year. From model year 1980, beginning with A = 1980, B = 1981, C = 1982, etc.
11	Places of production within the company: W = Wolfsburg N = Neckarsulm H = Hanover K = Osnabrück E = Emden M = Puebla, Mexico A = Ingolstadt V = Westmoreland, USA B = Brussels
12 – 17	Serial numbers, starting with 000 001 for each new model year.

Extras for the Beetle

In order to comply with the wishes of a wide range of customers in the various export markets, and with the licensing regulations applying in these countries, the Beetle has been supplied ex-works with the greatest possible variety of extras fitted. So far as possible chassis numbers have been included in the following lists so that the period of manufacture can readily be determined.

'M' extras, special features etc.

				Model
M 1	Chrome bumpers, hood flaps, exhaust pipes, front indicators, hood and door handles; also the trim and front passenger's sun visor			
	F	– –	117 999 000	111, 112
M 1	Torsion bar front axle, swing axle rear instead of suspension struts and dual suspension struts.			
	F 111 2000 001	– –	112 3200 000	113, 114
M 4	4-speed gearbox with dual suspension struts			USA, Canada
	F 159 000 001	– –	150 3100 000	151, 152
	F 119 000 001	– –		113, 114, 141-144
M 5	Saxomat 34 PS-Engine			
	M 5 000 001	– –	9 800 000	113, 114, 141-144, 151, 152
	M D 0 000 001	– –	D 0 095 049	111-114, 141-144, 151, 152
	M D 0 095 050	– –	D 0 234 014	111-114
M 6	Reinforced chassis in front axle area and strengthened torsion bars on rear			
	F 150 2141 186	– –	150 3100 000	151, 152
	F 110 2141 186	– –		113, 114, 141-144
M 9	Automatic gearbox 37 PS-Engine			
	M E 0 015 982	– –	E 0 020 100	M 59/M 87/M 240: 113, 114, 151, 152
	M E 0 020 101	– –	E 0 022 000	M 87/M 240: 113, 114, 151, 152
	40 PS-Engine			
	M F 1 462 599	– –	F 1 790 008	M 59/M 87: 113, 114, 151, 152
	M F 1 790 009	– –	F 2 200 000	M 87: 113, 114, 151, 152; M 52/M 610: 111, 112
	M L 0 019 430	– –	L 0 026 500	M 240: 113, 114, 141; 144, 151, 152
	M AC 0 000 001	– –		M 87/M 240: 113, 114; 1302, 1303; M 52/M 240/M 610: 111, 112
	44 PS-Engine			
	M H 0 879 927	– –	H 1 350 000	113, 114, 141; 144, 151, 152
	M H 5 077 366	– –	H 5 900 000	M 157: 113, 114, 141-144, 151, 152
	M AB 0 000 001	– –	AB 0 990 000	M 87: 113, 114; 1302, 1303;

M AR 0 000 001	– –		M 52/M 610: 111, 112
46 PS-Engine			
M AF 0 000 001	– –		M 240: 113, 114, 141; 144; 1302, 1303
47 PS-Engine			
M B 6 000 001	– –	B 6 600 000	M 157: 113, 114, 141-144, 151, 152
48 PS-Engine			
M AE 0 000 001	– –	AE 1 000 000	M 26/M 157: 113, 114, 141-144
M AE 0 000 001	– –	AE 0 917 263	M 26/M 157: 1302, 1303
M AE 0 917 264	– –	AE 1 000 000	1303: 133, 153
M AH 0 000 001	– –		M 26/M 27/M 157: 113, 114, 141-144
M AH 0 000 001	– –	AH 0 005 900	M 26/M 27/M 157: 1302, 1303
M AH 0 005 901	– –		M 27/103: 133, 153
M AK 0 000 001	– –		M 26/M 157: 113, 114, 141-144;
			1303: 133, 153
50 PS-Engine			
M AD 0 000 001	– –	AD 0 990 000	113, 114, 141-144
M AD 0 000 001	– –	AD 0 598 001	1302
M AD 0 598 002	– –	AD 0 990 000	1303: 135, 136, 151, 152
M AS 0 000 001	– –		113, 114, 141-144; 1303

M 9 Yellow tail lights — Australia, Italy

F   – –   146 1021 300   141-144

M 11 Sealed-beam headlamps, indicators with side marker
lights, red tail lights, hazard warning light system,
dual-circuit brake warning light, reversing lights, but
without headlight flasher parking lights or steering lock.   USA, Canada

F 148 000 001   – –   149 1200 000   141, 143

F 149 000 001   – –

(without hazard warning light system)
Sealed-beam headlamps, indicators with side marker
lights, red tail lights, buzzer for ignition switch, side
marker reflectors, reversing lights in brake/indicator
lights, dual circuit brake warning light, but without
headlight flasher, parking lights or steering wheel lock.

F 140 2000 001   – –   141 3200 000   141, 143

Sealed-beam headlamps, indicators with side marker
lights, red tail lights, buzzer for ignition switch, dual
circuit brake warning light, but without headlight
flasher, parking lights or steering wheel lock, also with

F 142 2000 001   – –   144 299 000   141, 143

horn for town use.

F 144 2000 001   – –   141, 143

M 12 Exhaust control — USA

F 115 2000 000   – –   117 2200 000   113

F 135 2000 001   – –   1303: 133, 153

F 115 2000 000   – –   115 2600 000   113

M 14 'Volkswagen' script badging — Export-markets
1302, 1303

F 116 000 001   – –   114 2999 000   113, 114, 151, 152

	F 156 000 001	– –	150 3100 000	141-144
	F 114 2000 001	– –	114 2999 000	111, 112
M 17	Fitting for lap-type seat belts			
	F	– –	116 1021 300	111-114, 151, 152
	F	– –	146 1021 300	141-144
M 18	Larger reflectors in brake indicator lights			Sweden
	F	– –	117 507 257	113, 114, 151, 152
M 19	without headlight flasher			
	F 116 000 001	– –	119 1200 000	113, 114, 141-144, 151, 152
	F 119 000 001	– –	119 1200 000	111-114, 141-144, 151, 152
	F 148 000 001	– –	159 1200 000	141-144
M 20	Speedometer marked in miles			Export-markets
M 21	Lockable outside door handles on both sides			Export-markets
	F 5 888 185	– –	6 502 399	113, 114, 151, 152
	F 115 000 001	– –	117 999 000	113, 114
M 22	Sealed-beam headlamps (sloping) with hazard warning light system			Export-markets Except USA
	F	– –	117 999 000	111-114, 151, 152
	Sealed-beam headlamps (vertical)			
	F 118 000 001	– –	119 1200 000	111-114, 151, 152
	Sealed-beam headlamps (vertical) and reversing light on bumper			
	F 110 2000 001	– –	113 2199 583	111, 112
	Sealed-beam headlamps (vertical) and reversing lights in brake/indicator lights			
	F 150 2000 001	– –	150 3100 000	151, 152
	F 110 2000 001	– –	114 2999 000	113, 114
	F 113 2199 584	– –	115 2600 000	111, 112
	F 111 2000 001	– –		1302; 1303: 135, 136, 151, 152
M 23	consisting of:			USA, Canada
	M 227 sealed-beam headlamps, indicators with side marker lights, red tail lights, dashboard covering and safety armrests, dual-circuit brake warning light, reversing lights in brake/indicator lights, but without headlamp flasher, parking lights or steering wheel lock			
	F 118 000 001	– –	119 1200 000	113, 151
	consisting of:			
	Sealed-beam headlamps, indicators with side marker lights, red tail lights, buzzer for ignition switch, side marker reflectors, reversing lights in brake/indicator lights, dashboard covering and safety armrests, dual-circuit brake warning light, but without headlamp flasher, parking lights or steering wheel lock			
	F 110 2000 001	– –	150 3100 000	113, 151
	F 111 2000 001			1302: 113, 151
M 26	Activated charcoal container for absorbing fuel fumes/ gases			USA, Canada, Japan
	F	– –		1302;
	F 110 2000 001	– –	115 2600 0000	113, 114

	F 150 2000	– – 150 3100 000	151, 152
	F 140 2000 001	– – 144 2999 000	141-144
	F 116 2000 001	– – 116 2200 000	111, 112
M 27	Compliance with exhaust regulations		Japan
	F 116 2071 468	– – 117 2200 000	112
M 27	Compliance with exhaust regulations for US West Coast		USA, West Coast
	F 112 2000 001	– – 117 2200 000	M 9/M 26/M 157: 113, 141, 143, 181
	F 133 2000 001	– –	1303: 133
	F 156 2108 077	– – 158 2039 687	153
M 27	Compliance with exhaust regulations for California		
	F 112 2000 1	– – 117 2200 000	M 157
	F 142 2000 1	– – 144 2999 000	
M 27	Lap-type seat belt inertia reel		USA, Canada
	F 117 000 001	– – 117 999 000	111-114, 151, 152
	F 147 000 001	– – 147 999 000	141-144
M 30	Headlight flasher with simultaneous number plate illumination		Austria
	F	– – 112 2427 792	111, 113, 151
	F	– – 112 2482 841	1302: 113, 151
	F	– – 142 2360 746	141, 143
M 32	Brake/indicator lights		Italy, Australia
	F	– – 4 010 994	111-114, 151, 152
M 32	Lockable cap for fuel tank		1303; 181
	F 113 2000 001	– –	111-114
	F 143 2000 001	– – 144 2999 000	141-142
M 34	Sidelight monitor lamp, side repeater indicators and reflectors		Italy
			1302, 1303
	F	– – 112 3200 000	111-114, 151, 152
	F 113 2000 001	– –	111, 113
	except:		
	F 116 000 001	– – 116 1021 300	111, 112
	with backrest locks on front seats		
M 34	Sidelight monitor lamp, and side repeater indicators Front indicators white/yellow and fitted with reflectors		Italy
	F	– – 142 3200 000	141-144
	F 143 2000 001	– –	141, 143
M 34	Indicators in front clear/amber, side repeater indicators, but without hazard warning light system		Italy
	F 135 2000 001	– – 135 2600 000	1303: 135
	F 155 2000 001	– – 157 2028 457	1303: 151
M 34	Side repeater indicator lights but no warning light system		Italy
	F 157 2029 458	– – 157 2060 038	1303: 151
M 34	Side repeater indicator lights, rear view mirror, but no hazard warning light system		
	F 157 2060 039	– –	1303: 151
M 36	Special bumpers		
	F 134 2000 001	– – 134 2999 000	1303: 135, 136, 151, 152

M 37	No hazard warning light system			Italy, France
		– –	134 2999 000	111-114, 141, 143, 151, 152, 181; 1302, 1303;
M 39	No seat or backrest in rear			
	F 115 2000 001	– –		111, 112
M 40	Speedometer with fuel gauge			
	F 110 2000 001	– –		111, 112
M 46	Side repeater indicators			Denmark, Norway, Italy
	F 111 2000 001	– –		111-114, 151, 152; 141-144;
	F 134 2000 001	– –		1302, 1303
M 47	Reversing lights on bumper			
	F 117 000 001	– –	117 999 000	111-114, 151, 152
	F 118 000 001	– –	113 2199 583	111, 112
	F 147 000 001	– –	149 1200 000	141-144
M 48	Front seat, official design			West German Post Office Police
	F 116 2000 001	– –		111, 112
M 50	Dual-circuit and handbrake check lights			
		– –	133 3200 000	1302: 113, 114, 151, 152;
	F 134 2000 001	– –	135 2600 000	1303: 135, 136;
	F 118 000 001	– –	113 3200 000	113, 114, 141-144
	F 113 2000 001	– –	113 3200 000	111, 112
M 52	37 PS-engine and compensating spring			
	F 118 000 001	– –	110 3100 000	M 240: 111, 112
	40 PS-engine and compensating spring			
	F 118 000 001	– –	110 3100 000	111, 112
	F 111 2000 001	– –	115 2600 000	M 240: 111, 112
	44 PS-engine and compensating spring			
	F 111 2000 001	– –	115 2600 000	111, 112
M 53	Cloth upholstery in place of leatherette			
	F 119 000 001	– –	113 3200 000	111, 112
M 54	Lockable glovebox lid			1302: 113, 114; 1303: 135, 136
	F 118 000 001	– –	114 2999 000	111-114
	F 149 000 001	– –		143, 144
	F 115 2000 001	– –	117 2200 000	M 108
M 55	Steering wheel lock with ignition/starter switch			Export (standard for home market)
	F 117 000 001	– –	119 1200 000	111-114, 141-144, 151, 152
M 55	Thermostatically controlled flap in rear engine hood			USA
	F 114 2000 001	– –	114 2999 000	M 108: 113
	F 134 2000 001	– –	134 2999 000	1303: 133, 153
M 58	Overriders on front and rear bumpers			
	F	– –	134 2999 000	1302; 1303: 135, 136, 151, 152
	F 110 2000 001	– –	114 2999 000	113, 114
	F 142 2000 001	– –		141- 144

M 59	Ignition/starter switch lock			Export (standard for home market)
	F	– –	146 1021 300	141-144
	Thermostatically controlled preheating for carburettor			Export-markets
	37 PS-Engine			
	M E 0 015 146	– –	E 0 020 100	M 52/M 240: 111, 112;
	40 PS-Engine			M 87/M 240: 113, 114; 151, 152
	M F 1 380 778	– –	F 1 790 008	M 52: 111, 112
	34 PS-Engine			M 87: 113, 114, 151,152
	M D 0 458 808	– –	D 0 540 002	111, 112
				M 88: 113, 114, 151, 152
M 60	Eberspächer stationary heater			111-114, 151, 152
				141, 143;
				1302, 1303
M 62	Washer reservoir with reduced air space and additional air take-off pipe; additional external rear view mirror, convex, on right			Sweden 111, 113, 151; 1302: 113, 151; 1303: 135, 151
M 62	Washer reservoir with reduced air space and additional air take-off pipe;			Sweden 141-144
	F 149 000 001	– –	140 3100 000	141, 143
	Additional external rear view mirror, convex, on right			113 (Sweden)
M 67	77 Ah battery, 6V			Export-markets
	F	– –	117 999 000	111-114, 151, 152
	F 118 000 001	– –		111, 112
M 69	Gun rack			181
M 74	Mudflaps, rear			111-114, 151, 152
				1302; 1303: 135, 136, 151, 152
M 79	Leatherette instead of cloth upholstery			
	F 114 2000 001	– –	115 2600 000	111, 112
M 80	Disc instead of drum brakes			
	F	– –	135 2600 000	M 87/1302;
				M 88/1302: 113, 114;
	F 159 000 001	– –	150 3100 000	M 87/1303: 135, 136, 151, 152;
				M 88/1303: 135, 136
	F 119 000 001	– –	114 2999 000	M 87, M 88: 113, 114, 151, 152
M 82	Mounting for first-aid box			
	F	– –	135 2600 000	1302, 1303;
	F 111 2000 001	– –	115 2600 000	111-114, 141-144
M 82	Side lenses in front indicators			Denmark
	F 116 463 103	– –	117 999 000	111-114, 151, 152
M 86	VW 1200, but without compensating spring			
	F 117 483 306	– –	117 999 000	M 129: 111, 112
M 86	Self-adjusting drum brakes			Sweden
	F 113 2000 001	– –	114 2999 000	1303: 135, 136, 151, 152;
				111-114, 141-144

M 87	37 PS-Engine			
	Single circuit drum brakes			
	F 117 000 001	– –	117 999 000	M 240: 113, 114, 151, 152
	Dual circuit drum brakes			
	F 118 000 001	– –	110 3100 000	111-114, 141-144, 151, 152
	40 PS-Engine			
	Single circuit drum brakes			
	F 117 000 001	– –	117 999 000	113, 114, 151, 152
	Dual circuit drum brakes			M 240/1302; M 240/1303;
	F 118 000 001	– –	110 3100 000	111-114, 141-144, 151, 152
	F 111 2000 001	– –	114 2999 000	M 240: 113, 114
	44 PS-Engine			
	Dual circuit drum brakes			1302; 1303: 135, 136, 151, 152
	F 111 2000 001	– –		113, 114
M 88	34 PS-Engine			
	Single circut drum brakes			113, 114, 151, 152
	F 117 000 001	– –	117 999 000	1302: 113, 114; 1303
	Dual circuit drum brakes			
	F 118 000 001	– –	114 2999 000	113, 114, 151, 152
M 89	Laminated windscreen			111-114, 141-144, 151, 152;
				1302; 1303: 135, 136, 151, 152; 181
M 93	Opening rear side windows			113, 114; 1302: 113, 114;
				1303: 133-136
M 94	Lockable rear engine cover			111-114, 151, 152;
				1302; 1303; 135, 136, 151, 152
M 102	Rear window heating			1302; 1303: 135, 136
	F 115 000 001	– –	117 999 000	111-114
	F 118 000 001	– –		113, 114
	F 110 2000 001	– –	115 2600 000	M 610: 111, 112
	F 150 2572 520	– –	150 3100 000	151, 152
	F 145 000 001	– –		143, 144
	F 149 862 321	– –		141, 142
M 103	Reinforced bumpers			111-114, 141-144, 151, 152;
				1302; 1303: 135, 136, 151, 152;
				211-274
M 105	Harder rubber/ metal bearings for transmission mountings			111-114, 141-144, 151, 152;
				1302; 1303
M 106	Special cloth upholstery			West German Post Office Police
				111-114
M 107	Anti-collision protection			
	F	– –	117 999 000	113, 114, 151, 152
	F 118 000 001	– –	110 3100 000	111, 112
	F	– –	141 3200 000	141-144
	F	– –	156 2000 000	151-153
M 108	Custom model with torsion bar front axle instead of MacPherson struts; also with M 4 or M 9, M 20, M 23, M 89, M 137, M 185, M 227, M 228, M 617			USA

207

	F 111 2000 001	– –	117 2200 000	113
	(F 112 2000 001	– –	117 2200 000	
	but without M 617)			
M 110	Synchromesh gears, hydraulic brakes; also with trim strips			Canada
	F	– –	4 630 937	111
	Fully synchronised gears; also trim strips, but without external mirror			
	F 4 630 938	– –	116 1021 300	111
	With M 129; also with trim strips, PVC-lined luggage space, but without external mirror			
	F 117 000 001	– –	117 999 000	111
	With M 20, M 23, M 60, M 88, M 89, M 227, M 617; Custom model 113			
	PVC lining in footwells and luggage space, but without compensating spring or fresh air ventilation; no ashtrays in side panels			
	F 112 2000 001	– –		
	but without M 617			
	F 118 000 001	– –	114 2999 00	113
M 113	Security system			Canada
	F 135 2000 001	– –		1303: 133, 153
M 121	Air blower for ventilation			
	F 111 2000 001	– –	114 2999 000	1302: 113, 114;
	F 116 2000 001	– –		1303: 135, 136;
				113, 114
M 123	Special remote inteference suppression			France
				111-114, 141-144, 181
				151, 152; 1302, 1303
M 124	Amber headlamps and safety rear view mirror			Export-markets
				111-114, 141- 144, 151, 152;
				181, 1302; 1303: 135, 136, 151, 152
M 129	34 PS-Engine			
	F 117 000 001	– –	117 999 000	111, 112
M 132	Deformable section			except for UK, France, Sweden
	F 133 2683 042	– –		1303: 135, 136, 151, 152
M 137	Dual-circuit drum brakes			Export-markets
		– –		1302; 1303
	F 117 000 001	– –	117 999 000	113, 114, 141-144, 151, 152
	F 118 000 001	– –	110 3100 000	113, 114, 151, 152
M 138	Sealed-beam headlamps, red tail lights, hazard warning system, but without headlight flasher			Export-markets
	F	– –	147 999 000	141-144
	Sealed-beam headlamps, red tail lights, but without headlight flasher			
	F 148 000 001	– –	149 1200 000	141-144
	Sealed-beam headlamps, front indicator lights with side			

markers, reflectors in brake/indicator lights, red tail lights

F 140 2000 001	– –	141 3200 000	141-144

Sealed-beam headlamps, front indicator lights with side markers, red rear lights

F 142 2000 001	– –	141 3200 000	141-144

Sealed-beam headlamps, front indicator lights with side markers

F 143 2000 001	– –		141-144

M 139   Dual-circuit drum brakes   Canada, Scandinavia

F 117 000 001	– –	119 1200 000	111, 112

M 149   Painted instead of chrome parts

F 118 000 001	– –		111, 112
F 111 2000 001	– –	114 2999 000	113, 114
F	– –	112 3200 000	1302: 113, 114
F 133 2000 001	– –	135 2600 000	1303: 135, 136

M 153   Oil bath air filter with initial cyclone filter

F	– –	115 999 000	111-114, 141-144

M 153   Double oilbath air filter system   Export-markets
1302: 113, 114;
1303: 135, 136

F 116 000 001	– –	110 3100 000	111-114, 141-144
F 111 2000 001	– –		111, 114

M 157   44 PS-engine with exhaust gas purification system   USA, Canada

M H 5 000 001	– –	H 5 900 000	113, 114, 141-144, 151, 152

47 PS-engine with exhaust gas purification system

M B 6 000 001	– –	B 600 000	113, 114, 141-144, 151, 152

48 PS-engine with exhaust gas purification system

M AE 0 558 001	– –	AE 1 000 000	113, 141, 143

50 PS-engine with exhaust gas purification system

M AE 0 000 001	– –	AE 0 558 000	113, 141, 143

48 PS-engine with exhaust gas purification system and activated charcoal container for absorbing fuel gases/fumes

M AE 0 000 001	– –	AE 0 917 263	1302
M AH 0 000 001	– –	AH 0 005 900	1302
M AH 0 000 001	– –		M 27: 113, 141, 143
M AK 0 000 001	– –	AK 0 239 493	113, 141, 143, 133, 153

50 PS injection engine with exhaust gas purification system and activated charcoal container for absorbing fuel gases/fumes   USA, Canada

M AJ 0000 001	– –	AJ 0 119 687	M 108, M 307; Japan: M 193/M 599
M AJ 0071 683	– –	AJ 0 119 687	112

M 162   Rubber strips on bumpers   113, 114;
1302: 113, 114;
1303; 135, 136

M 167   88 Ah battery   USA

F	– –	117 999 000	113, 114, 141-144, 151, 152

M 167   Additional grab handle and coat hooks

F 113 2000 001	– –		111, 112

M 168	Enlarged external rear view mirror and additional switch for inside light			147
M 179	Locking device for front seat backrest			
	F 117 000 001	– –	112 3200 000	111, 112
M 183	Lap belt for rear seat (non automatic)			West Germany
	F 159 2027 869	– –		1303: 151, 152
M 184	Three-point safety belt for front seat			USA; 111, 112
M 185	Three-point safety belt for front seat and (automatic) lap belt for rear			113
	F 112 2360 221	– –	117 2200 3000	
M 186	Lap belt for back seat			USA, Canada
	F 118 096 786	– –	112 2360 220	113, 151
	F 118 096 786	– –	112 3200 000	113, 151
M 186	Lap belt for rear seat (automatic)			not for USA
	F 112 2360 221	– –		111-114
M 187	Headlamps for right-hand drive			right-hand drive Model 141-144; 1302; 1303: 135, 136, 151, 152; 111-114, 151, 152
M 190	Increased door security			USA
	F 113 2438 834	– –	114 2999 000	113; M 108
	F 143 2401 303	– –		141-144
	F 133 2438 834	– –	135 2600 000	1303: 135
M 193	Compliance with laws concerning exhaust emissions and electrical equipment			Japan
	F 114 2000 001	– –		112-114
	F 144 2000 001	– –		142, 144
	F 134 2000 001	– –	156 2108 076	1303: 135, 136, 152
	F 156 2108 077	– –	158 2039 687	1303: 151
M 194	External convex rear view mirrors, left and right (konvex)			West German Post Office 112
M 206	Anti-dazzle internal rear view mirror			1302: 113, 114; 1303: 135, 136; 141-144
	F 159 000 001	– –	150 3100 000	151, 152
	F 119 000 001	– –		113, 114
	F 111 2000 001	– –		111, 112
M 208	Electrical installation for trailer towing			
	F 112 2000 001	– –	114 2999 000	113, 114
	F 112 2000 001	– –	115 2600 000	111, 112
	F 112 2000 001	– –	135 2600 000	1302, 1303: 135, 136 151, 152

M 218	Wheel trims			
	F 117 000 001	– –	119 1200 000	113, 114
M 220	Locking differential			111-114, 141-144, 151, 152;
				1302; 1303: 135, 136, 151, 152; 181
M 227	High-back front seat (head support)			
	F	– –	135 2600 000	1302; 1303: 135, 136, 151, 152;
	F 118 000 001	– –		113, 114, 151, 152
	F 112 2000 001	– –	115 2999 000	111, 112
	F 148 000 001	– –	144 2999 000	141-144
M 228	Dashboard covering			
	F 119 000 001	– –	110 3100 000	113, 151
	F 111 2000 001	– –		113, 114; M 23, M 108, M 110,
				M 602, M 603
	F 114 2000 001	– –		111
	F 149 000 001	– –	141 3200 000	141-144
	F	– –	112 3200 000	1302: 113, 114
M 231	Reclining seat for front passenger			181
M 232	Lockable covers for front and rear seats			
	F	– –	112 3200 000	1302: 151
M 233	VW 1303 with lower specification, similar to Model 1200			1303: 135, 136
M 240	Engine with dished pistons for lower octane fuel (Identified by 'E' in front of engine number, on 37 hp unit)			
	F 116 000 001	– –	116 1021 300	113, 114, 141-144, 151, 152
	F 117 000 001	– –	117 999 000	111, 112;
				M 87: 113, 114, 151, 152
	F 118 000 001	– –	110 3100 000	M 52: 111, 112,
				M 87: 113, 114, 151, 152
	(Identified by 'L' in front of engine number, on 40 hp unit)			
	F 117 000 001	– –	110 3100 000	113, 114, 141-144, 151, 152
	(Identified by 'AC' in front of engine number, on 46 hp)			
	F 111 2000 001	– –		M 87: 113, 114;
				M 52: 111, 112
	(Identified by 'AF' in front of engine number, on 46 hp)			
	F 111 2000 001	– –		113, 114, 141-144
	(Identified by 'AC' in front of engine number, on 40 hp)			M 87/1302;
				M 87/1303: 135, 136, 151, 152
	(Identified by 'AF' in front of engine number, on 46 hp)			1302; 1303;
				135, 136, 151, 152
M 248	Ignition/starter switch without steering wheel lock			Export-markets
	F	– –	135 2600 000	1302; 1303: 135, 136, 151, 152;
	F 110 2000 001	– –	115 2600 000	111-114, 141-144, 151, 152
M 258	Adjustable headrests			Export-markets
	F 113 2000 001	– –	117 2200 000	M 108: 113;
	F 117 2000 001	– –		111, 112
	F 156 2000 001	–	–	1303: 151, 152

M 261	Additional external rear view mirror on right, flat			
	F	– –	155 2600 000	1302: 151
				1303: 151
	F 118 000 001	– –	150 3100 000	141, 143, 151
M 277	Rear engine cover without air vents			Switzerland
	F 113 2000 001	– –	114 2999 000	M 87: 113, 135, 136, 151, 152
	F 115 2000 001	– –	115 2600 000	M 52: 111, 112
M 282	Sun visor for front passenger			
	F 111 2000 001	– –		111, 112
M 288	Headlamp washers			
	F 114 2000 001	– –	114 2999 000	113, 114
	F 134 2000 001	– –		1303
M 289	Shearable screw for steering column fastening			Denmark
				1302; 1303:
				135, 136, 151, 152;
	F 112 2000	– –	114 2718 376	111-114
	F 142 2001	– –	144 2999 000	141-144
M 307	Basic model with torsion bar front axle:			USA, Canada
	For USA equipped with M 4, M 12, M 85, M 137, M 157,			
	M 185, M 190, M 227, M 228, M 253;			
	For Canada equipped with M 4, M 20, M 23, M 85, M 89,			
	M 113, M 137, M 185, M 190, M 227, M 228, M 253			
	F 115 2000 001	– –	115 2600 000	
M 335	37 kW (50 PS) engine, 1.6 litre			Austria
	F 116 2000 001	– –		M 599: 111, 112
	F 156 2000 001	– –		1303: 151
M 409	Sports style front seats in black cloth			
	F 113 2000 001	– –	114 2999 000	113, 114
	F 133 2000 001	– –	135 2600 000	1303
M 416	Safety steering wheel			Austria, Switzerland,
	F 115 2000 001	– –		Japan, Australia
				111, 112
M 444	Wheels 5$\frac{1}{2}$J x 15, sports style			
	F 133 2000 001	– –		1303: 135, 136, 151, 152
M 527	With exhaust emission control			Japan, Sweden
	F	– –	111 3200 000	113, 114, 141-144, 151, 152
				M 87: 113, 114, 151, 152;
				M 88/M 610: 111, 112
M 527	With exhaust emission control			Japan, Sweden
	F	– –	111 3200 000	1302; M 87/1302
M 528	Additional external rear view mirror on right, convex			
				1302: 113, 151;
				1303: 135, 151;
	F 119 000 001	– –	114 2999 000	111, 113, 151
	F 149 000 001	– –		141, 143

M 531	Harder torsion bars at rear			
	F 141 2000 001	– –	144 2999 000	141-144
	F 111 2000 001	– –	114 2999 000	
M 549	Three-point safety belt for front seat			not for USA, Canada
	F 134 2000 001	– –		1303: 135, 136, 151, 152
	F 114 2000 001	– –		111-114
M 551	Halogen headlamps (instead of tungsten)			
	F 118 000 001	– –	114 2999 000	113, 114, 151, 152
	F 112 2299 679	– –	112 3200 000	1302
	F 133 2000 001	– –		1303: 135, 136, 151, 152
M 559	Front valance with air vents			1302, 1303
M 560	Steel wind-back roof			111-114;
				1302: 113, 114;
				1303: 133-136
M 562	Reclining seat			1303: 135, 136;
	F 113 2000 001	– –	114 2999 000	113, 114
	F 114 2000 001	– –	115 2600 000	M 603: 111, 112
M 563	Arm rest in back seat			
M 565	Sports steering wheel			1303
	F 112 2000 001	– –		113, 114, 141-144
M 568	Heat-insulating glass in door quarter, side and rear windows			
	F 134 2000 001	– –	135 2600 000	1303: 133-136
	F 114 2000 001	– –	114 2600 000	111-114
M 568	Green-tinted glass all round			
	F 116 2000 001	– –		111-114
M 571	Rear fog light			1302; 1303: 135, 136, 151, 152;
	F 113 2000 001	– –	114 2999 000	113, 114
	F 142 2360 186	– –		141-144
M 599	50 PS engine with disc brakes and compensating spring			
	F 114 2000 001	– –		111, 112
M 601	De luxe equipment			
	F 118 000 001	– –	118 1016 100	113, 114, 151, 152
M 601	De luxe equipment			
	F 148 000 001	– –	148 999 000	141-144
	consisting of:			
	M 47 Reversing lights;			
	M 102 heated rear window (143,			
	144 only)			
	Hazard warning light system dual-circuit brake			
	warning light, tray below dashboard			
M 602	De luxe equipment			
	F 118 000 001	– –	118 1016 100	111-114, 151, 152

M 602	Luxury equipment			
	F 148 000 001	– –	148 999 000	141-144
	consisting of:			
	Hazard light system, dual-circuit brake warning lights,			
	tray below dashboard			
				USA, Canada
M 602	Luxury equipment			1302: 113
M 602	Luxury equipment			
	consisting of:			
	Hazard warning light system, dual-circuit brake			
	warning light and padded dashboard			
M 603	Luxury equipment			
	F 110 2000 001	– –	114 2999 000	113
	F 111 2000 001	– –	114 2999 000	114
	F 114 2000 001	– –		111, 112
	F	– –	112 3200 000	1302: 113, 114
	F 133 2000 001	– –	134 2999 000	1303: 135, 136
	Halogen double filament headlamps (HI lamps)			
M 607	Windscreen wiper with 2-speed 12V motor			Norway
	F 111 2518 856	– –	113 3200 00	M 610: 111
M 607	Windscreen wiper with 2-speed 12V motor and locking			Norway
	back rest for rear seat			
	F 114 2000 001	– –	115 2600 000	M 610: 111
M 607	Windscren wiper with 2-speed 12V motor and locking			Norway
	back rest for rear seat			
	F 116 2000 001		115 2600 000	M 610: 111
M 608	Three-point safety belts for front seat (automatic)			Australia
	F 115 2143 744	– –	116 2200 000	112
	F 135 2143 744	– –	135 2600 000	1303: 136
M 610	12V system			
	F	– –	117 999 000	111-114, 141-144, 151, 152
	F 118 000 001	– –		111, 112
M 611	12V system, sealed-beam headlamps (vertical), and			Export-markets
	hazard warning system			
	F 117 000 001	– –	117 999 000	111-114, 151, 152
	F 118 000 001	– –		
	(without hazard warning system)			
M 613	12V system with interference suppression			Police
				1302: 113, 114;
				1303: 135, 136
	F 116 000 001	– –	117 999 000	111. 114
	F 118 000 001	– –		113, 114, M 610: 111, 112
M 616	Reversing lights in brake indicator lights			
				1302: 113, 114;
				1303: 135, 136;
	F 118 000 001	– –	110 3100 000	113, 114, 151, 152
	F 111 2000 001	– –		113, 114

	F 113 2000 001	– –		111, 112
	F 140 2000 001	– – 141 3200 000		141-144
M 617	Washer reservoir with reduced air space and additional air take-off pipe			
	F 118 000 001	– – 110 3100 000		111-114, 141-144, 151, 152
M 618	Alternator, 12V, 50A			USA
	M AH 0 042 350	– – AH 0 066 648		M 27/M 618: 113, 141, 143, 133, 153
	M AH 0 057 246	– – AH 0 075 453		M 9/ M 27/M 618: 113, 141, 143, 133, 153
	M AK 0 061 082	– – AK 0 239 364		M 157/M 618: 113, 141, 143; M 618: 133, 153
	M AF 0 036 743	– – AF 0 036 768		M 240/M618 113, 114, 135, 136, 141-144, 151, 152
	M AD 0 878 890	– – AD 0 990 000		M 618: 113, 114 135, 136, 141-144, 151, 152
M 622	Cigarette lighter			1303: 133-136, 153
M 652	Interval relay for windscreen wiper			1302; 1303; 135, 136, 151, 152;
	F 112 2000 001	– – 114 2999 000		113, 114, 141-144
M 649	Lap belt attachment points for three persons in back seat			
	F 115 2143 744	– –		111, 112
M 659	Halogen fog lights			1302; 1303: 135, 136, 151, 152
	F 112 2427 793	– – 114 2999 000		113, 114
	F 112 2427 793	– – 115 2600 000		M 610: 111, 112
	F 116 2000 001	– –		111, 112
M 671	Heat insulating laminated windscreen			
	F 134 2000 001	– – 135 2600 000		1303: 133-136
	F 114 2000 001	– – 114 29990 000		111-114
M 676	Clock			1303
M 976	Sports style wheels			
		– –		1303
	F 143 2000 001	– – 144 2999 000		141-144
	F 113 2000 001	– – 114 2999 000		113, 144
	F 113 2000 001	– –		111, 112
S 759	Dual-circuit disc brakes			Scandinavia
	F 117 000 001	– – 117 999 000		113, 114
S 760	Dual-circuit drum brakes			Scandinavia
	F 117 000 001	– – 117 999 000		M 87: 113, 114, 151, 152

Special models

S 708	Special wrap-around rear bumpers			USA
	F 116 2006 148	– – 117 2200 000		M 108, 113

S 710	Brake lights amber/red instead of amber/ red/clear		West German Post Office
	F 114 2565 674	– – 115 2049 312	111-114
S 714	Special trim and paint		Export-markets
	F 113 2199 639	– – 113 3200 000	111-114; M 108
S 714	'The Yellow and Black Racer'		
	F 133 2199 639	– – 133 3200 000	1303: 133, 135
	F 113 2199 639	– – 113 3200 000	111-114; M 108
S 714	'Jeans 74'		Inland
	F 114 2489 588	– – 114 2999 000	111
S 715	'Love Bug'		USA
	F 114 2663 306	– – 114 2999 000	M 108
S 715	'Leisure Beetle'		Inland
	F 115 2143 744	– – 115 2600 000	111
S 716	'Jeans 74'		Export
	F 114 2489 588	– – 114 2999 000	111, 112
S 716	Steering column, steering column shroud, combination switch, steering wheel		Inland
	F 116 2098 785	– –	M 603: 111
S 717	'1200 L Herringbone'		Inland
	F 114 2489 588	– – 114 2999 000	M 603: 111
S 719	'1200 L Herringbone'		Export
	F 114 2489 588	– – 144 2999 000	M 603: 111, 112
S 729	'Luxury Beetle'		Export-markets not for USA, Canada
	F 134 2565 674	– – 134 2772 768	1303: 135, 136
S 723	Special for USA		USA
	F 157 2067 784	– –	1303: 135
			USA, Canada
	F 134 2423 796	– – 134 2565 673	1303:, 133, 153
	F 135 2248 016	– – 135 2248 083	1303: 133
	F 135 2262 066	– – 135 2600 000	1303: 133
S 736	'Sun Beetle'		USA, Canada
	F 114 2423 796	– – 114 2999 000	M 108, M 110
S 736	'Spring Messenger'		Inland
	F 113 2606 864	– – 113 3200 000	111
	F 133 2606 864	– – 133 3200 000	1303: 135
S 736	'Luxury Beetle'		USA, Canada
	F 135 2000 001	– – 135 2187 424	1303: 133
S 739	Special for USA		USA
	F 156 2078 287	– – 156 2200 000	1303: 153
S 744	'Jeans III'		
	F 115 2020 344	– – 115 2600 000	111, 112

S 759	'Black is Beautiful'			Export, not USA, Canada
	F 113 2606 864	– –	133 3200 000	111-114
	F 133 2606 864	– –	133 3200 000	1303: 135, 136
S 761	'Jeans Bug'			
	F 114 2000 001	– –	114 2423 795	111, 112
S 763	'Big Bug'			
	F 134 2000 001	– –	134 2356 316	1303: 135, 136
S 764	'City Bug'			
	F 134 2000 001	– –	134 2356 316	1303: 135, 136
S 765	'Champagne Edition II'			USA
	F 158 2033 080	– –	158 2057 289	1303: 153
S 785	'Spring Messenger'			Export, not USA, Canada
	F 113 2606 864	– –	113 3200 000	113, 114
	F 133 2606 864	– –	133 3200 000	1303: 135, 136

S 700	VW 1200 with outside painted bright yellow, interior fittings curry (1984)	West Germany
S 701	'Velvet-red Beetle'. Outside paintwork velvet red, seat material red and blue (1984)	West Germany
S 703	'Silver Bug' (1981)	West Germany
S 704	'Jeans Bug' (1982)	West Germany
S 706	'Special Bug' (1982)	West Germany
S 707	'Aubergine Beetle' with paintwork metallic aubergine, inside trim aubergine (1983)	West Germany
S 708	VW 1200 with paintwork Metallic Ice Blue, inside trim grey-blue (1983)	West Germany
S 710	VW 1200 with paintwork Alpine White, inside trim aubergine (1983)	West Germany
S 711	VW 1200 with paintwork Alpine White, inside trim grey-blue (1982)	West Germany

Engine identification letters

From 1 August 1965 an identifying letter was placed in front of engine numbers. If an X or two arrows (⟳) appear before an engine number this indicates a replacement power unit. The engine number appears beneath the dynamo mounting.

D	34 PS/25kW 1.2 l capacity from 1.8.65
F	40 PS/29kW 1.3 l capacity from 1.8.65 to 7.70
H	44 PS/32 kW 1.5 l capacity from 1.8.66 to 7.70
AB	44 PS/32 kW 1.3 l capacity from 8.70 to 31.7.73
AR	44 PS/32 kW 1.3 l capacity from 1.8.73 to 31.7.75
AD	50 PS/37 kW 1.6 l capacity from 1.8.70 to 7.73
AS	50 PS/37 kW 1.6 l capacity 1.8.73 to 10.1.80

Export markets

B	47 PS/35 kW 1.6 l capacity from 8.68 to 7.70, USA
E	37 PS/27 kW) 1.3 l capacity from 8.67 to 7.70
L	40 PS/29 kW 1.5 l capacity from 8.67 to 7.70
AC	40 PS/29 kW[1]) 1.3 l capacity from 8.70 to 7.72
AE	47 PS/35 kW 1.6 l capacity from 8.70 to 7.71, USA
AF	46 PS/34 kW[1]) 1.6 l capacity from 8.70 to 12.77
AH	47 PS/35 kW 1.6 l capacity from 8.71 to 1.76, USA
AJ	50 PS/37 kW 1.6 l capacity from 8.74 to 12.77, USA Japan, L-Jetronic
AK	47 PS/35 kW 1.6 l capacity from 8.72 to 7.73, USA

Engine data, with engine and chassis numbers

Year	Chassis No.		Engine No.	
1940	from 1–00001	to 1–01000	from 1–00001	to 1–01000
1941	from 1–01001	to 1–05656	from 1–01001	to 1–06251
1942	from 1–05657	to 1–014383	from 1–06252	to 1–017113
1943	from 1–014384	to 1–0032302	from 1–017114	to 1–045707
1944	from 1–032303	to 1–051999	from 1–045708	to 1–077682
1945	from 1–052000	to 1–053814	from 1–077683	to 1–079093
1946	from 1–053815	to 1–063796	from 1–079094	to 1–090732
1947	from 1–063797	to 1–072743	from 1–090733	to 1–0100788

Model years 1947 – 1951

	31. Dec. 1947	31. Dec. 1948	31. Dec. 1949	31. Dec. 1950	31. Dec. 1951
Engines	Engine no.	Engine no.	Engine no.	Engine no.	Engine no.
1.2 litre 18 kW (25 PS)	100788	122649	169913	265999	379470
Chassis Nos.	072743	091921	138554	220133	313829

Model years 1952 – 1953

	1. Oct. 1952	31. Dec. 1952	31. Mar. 1953	31. Dec. 1953	
Engines	Engine no.	Engine no.	Engine no.	Engine no.	
1.2 litre 18 kW (25 PS)	481713	519258	551113	695281*)	
Chassis Nos.	397023	428156	454951	575414	

* Final number of series

Model years 1954 – 1955

	1. Jan. 1954	31. Dec. 1954	1. Aug. 1955	31. Dec. 1955	
Engines	Engine no.	Engine no.	Engine no.	Engine no.	
1.2 litre 22 kW (30 PS)	695282	945526	1120615	1277347	
Chassis Nos.	575415	781884	929746	1060929	

Model years 1956 – 1957

Engines	31. Dec. 1956 Engine no.	1. Aug. 1957 Engine no.	31. Dec. 1957 Engine no.		
1.2 litre 22 kW (30 PS)	1 678 209	1 937 450	2 156 321		
Chassis Nos.	1 394 119	1 600 440	1 774 680		

Model years 1958 – 1960

Engines	31. Dec.1958 Engine no.	1. Aug. 1959 Engine no.	31. Dec. 1959 Engine no.	31. July 1960 Engine no.	
1.2 litre 22 kW (30 PS)	2 721 313	3 072 320	3 424 453	3 912 903	
Chassis Nos.	2 226 206	2 528 668	2 801 613	3 192 506	

Model year 1961

Engines	1. Aug. 1960 Engine no.	31. Dec. 1960 Engine no.	31. July 1961 Engine no.		
1.2 litre 22 kW (30 PS) 1.2 litre 25 kW (34 PS)	3 912 904 5 000 001	3 915 041 5 428 637	3 924 022 5 958 947		
Chassis Nos.	3 192 507	3 551 044	4 010 994		

Model year 1962

Engines	1. Aug. 1961 Engine no.	31. Dec. 1961 Engine no.	1. July 1962 Engine no.		
1.2 litre 22 kW (30 PS) 1.2 litre 25 kW (34 PS)	3 924 023 5 958 948	3 931 468 6 375 945	3 942 914 6 935 203		
Chassis Nos.	4 010 995	4 400 051	4 846 835		

Model year 1963

Engines	1. Aug. 1962 Engine no.	31. Dec. 1962 Engine no.	31. July 1963 Engine no.		
1.2 litre 22 kW (30 PS)	3 942 915	3 949 223	3 959 303		
1.2 litre 25 kW (34 PS)	6 935 204	7 336 420	7 893 118		
Chassis Nos.	4 846 836	5 225 042	5 677 118		

Model year 1964

Engines	1. Aug. 1963 Engine no.	31. Dec. 1963 Engine no.	31. July 1964 Engine no.		
1.2 litre 22 kW (30 PS)	3 959 304	3 965 218	3 972 440		
1.2 litre 25 kW (34 PS)	7 893 119	8 264 628	8 796 622		
Chassis Nos.	5 677 119	6 016 120	6 502 399		

Model year 1965

Engines	1. Aug. 1964 Engine no.	31. Dec. 1964 Engine no.	31. July 1965 Engine no.		
1.2 litre 22 kW (30 PS)	3 972 441	3 984 729	4 050 000*)		
1.2 litre 25 kW (34 PS)	8 796 623	9 339 890	9 800 000		
Chassis Nos.	115 000 001	115 410 000	115 999 000		

1 Final number of series

Model year 1966

Engines	1. Aug. 1965 Engine no.	31. Dec. 1965 Engine no.	31. July 1966 Engine no.		
1.2 litre 25 kW (34 PS)	D 0 000 001	D 0 050 314	D 0 095 049		
1.3 litre 27 kW (37 PS)	E 0 000 001	E 0 002 999	E 0 006 000		
1.3 litre 29 kW (40 PS)	F 0 000 001	F 0 442 242	F 0 940 716		
Chassis Nos.	116 000 001	116 463 103	116 1021 300		

Model year 1967

Engines	1. Aug. 1966 Engine no.	31. Dec. 1966 Engine no.	31. July 1967 Engine no.		
1.2 litre 25 kW (34 PS)	D 0 095 050	D 0 120 750	D 0 234 014		
1.3 litre 27 kW (37 PS)	E 0 006 001	E 0 011 444	E 0 014 000		
1.3 litre 29 kW (40 PS)	F 0 940 717	F 1 057 754	F 1 237 506		
1.5 litre 29 kW (40 PS)	L 0 000 001	L 0 011 930	L 0 019 336		
1.5 litre 32 kW (44 PS)	H 0 204 001	H 0 576 613	H 0 874 199		
Chassis Nos.	117 000 001	117 442 503	117 999 000		

Model year 1968

Engines	1. Aug. 1967 Engine no.	31. Dec. 1967 Engine no.	31. July 1968 Engine no.		
1.2 litre 25 kW (34 PS)	D 0 234 015	D 0 297 008	D 0 382 979		
1.3 litre 27 kW (37 PS)	E 0 014 001	E 0 014 311	E 0 015 981		
1.3 litre 29 kW (40 PS)	F 1 237 507	F 1 296 298	F 1 462 598		
1.5 litre 29 kW (40 PS)	L 0 019 337	L 0 020 200	L 0 021 115		
1.5 litre 32 kW (44 PS)	H 0 874 200	H 0 915 221	H 1 003 255		
1.5 litre 32 kW (44 PS) (M 157)	H 5 000 001	H 5 173 897	H 5 414 585		
Chassis Nos.	118 000 001	118 431 603	118 1016 100		

Model year 1969

Engines	1. Aug. 1968 Engine no.	31. Dec. 1968 Engine no.	31. July 1969 Engine no.		
1.2 litre 25 kW (34 PS)	D 0 382 980	D 0 438 824	D 0 525 049		
1.3 litre 27 kW (37 PS)	E 0 015 982	E 0 018 367	E 0 020 021		
1.3 litre 29 kW (40 PS)	F 1 462 599	F 1 592 024	F 1 778 163		
1.5 litre 29 kW (40 PS)	L 0 021 116	L 0 021 903	L 0 024 106		
1.5 litre 32 kW (44 PS)	H 1 003 256	H 1 057 844	H 1 124 668		
1.5 litre 32 kW (44 PS) (M 157)	H 5 414 586	H 5 648 888	H 5 900 000		
Chassis Nos.	119 000 001	119 474 780	119 1200 000		

Model year 1970

Engines	1. Aug. 1969 Engine no.	31. Dec. 1969 Engine no.	31. July 1970 Engine no.		
1.2 litre 25 kW (34 PS)	D 0 525 050	D 0 592 445	D 0 674 999		
1.3 litre 27 kW (37 PS)	E 0 020 022	E 0 020 937	E 0 022 000*)		
1.3 litre 29 kW (40 PS)	F 1 778 164	F 1 932 908	F 2 200 000*)		
1.5 litre 29 kW (40 PS)	L 0 024 107	L 0 024 788	L 0 026 500*)		
1.5 litre 32 kW (44 PS)	H 1 124 669	H 1 187 829	H 1 350 000*)		
1.6 litre 35 kW (47 PS)	B 6 000 001	B 6 192 532	B 6 600 000*)		
Chassis Nos.	110 2 000 001	110 2 473 153	110 3 100 000		

* Final number of series

Model year 1971

Engines	1. Aug. 1970 Engine no.	31. Dec. 1970 Engine no.	31. July 1971 Engine no.		
1.2 litre 25 kW (34 PS)	D 0 675 000	D 0 719 487	D 0 835 006		
1.3 litre 29 kW (40 PS)	AC 0 000 001	AC 0 000 706	AC 0 003 239		
1.3 litre 32 kW (44 PS)	AB 0 000 001	AB 0 141 591	AB 0 350 000		
1.6 litre 34 kW (46 PS)	AF 0 000 001	AF 0 000 247	AF 0 000 444		
1.6 litre 37 kW (50 PS)	AD 0 000 001	AD 0 139 549	AD 0 360 022		
1.6 litre 37 kW (50 PS) (M 157)	AE 0 000 001	AE 0 218 430	AE 0 558 000		
Chassis Nos.	111 2 000 001	111 2 427 591	111 3 200 000		

Model year 1972

Engines	1. Aug. 1971 Engine no.	31. Dec. 1971 Engine no.	31. July 1972 Engine no.		
1.2 litre 25 kW (34 PS)	D 0 835 007	D 0 881 604	D 1 000 000		
1.3 litre 29 kW (40 PS)	AC 0 003 240	AC 0 005 192	AC 0 006 700		
1.3 litre 32 kW (44 PS)	AB 0 350 001	AB 0 447 700	AB 0 699 001		
1.6 litre 34 kW (46 PS)	AF 0 000 445	AF 0 000 654	AF 0 000 801		
1.6 litre 35 kW (48 PS)	AE 0 558 001	AE 0 727 810	AE 0 917 263		
1.6 litre 35 kW (48 PS) (M 157)	AH 0 000 001	AH 0 002 731	AH 0 005 900		
1.6 litre 37 kW (50 PS)	AD 0 360 023	AD 0 363 001	AD 0 598 001		
Chassis Nos.	112 2 000 000	112 2 427 792	112 3 200 000		

Model year 1973

Engines	1. Aug. 1972 Engine no.	1. Oct 1972 Engine no.	31. Dec. 1972 Engine no.	31. July 1973 Engine no.	
1.2 litre 25 kW (34 PS)	D 1 000 001		D 1 039 792	D 1 115 873	
1.3 litre 29 kW (40 PS)	AC 0 006 701		AC 0 007 219	AC 0 008 195	
1.3 litre 32 kW (44 PS)	AB 0 699 002		AB 0 820 427	AB 0 990 000	
1.6 litre 34 kW (46 PS)	AF 0 000 802		AF 0 034 850	AF 0 036 768	
1.6 litre 35 kW (48 PS)	AE 0 917 264	AE 1 000 000			
1.6 litre 35 kW		AK 0 000 001	AK 0 060 039	AK 0 239 364	
(48 PS/M 27)		AH 0 033 404			
1.6 litre 37 kW (50 PS)	AH 0 005 901		AH 0 056 934	AH 0 114 418	
	AD 0 598 002		AD 0 749 789	AD 0 990 000	
Chassis Nos.(VW 1303)	133 2000 001	———	133 2438 833	133 3200 000	
Chassis Nos.	113 2000 001	113 2212 117	113 2438 833	113 3200 000	

Model year 1974

Engines	1. Aug. 1973 Engine no.	31. Dec. 1973 Engine no.	31. July 1974 Engine no.		
1.2 litre 25 kW (34 PS)	D 1 115 874	D 1 204 346	D 1 284 226		
1.3 litre 32 kW (44 PS)	AR 000 001	AR 081 514	AR 121 271		
1.6 litre 37 kW (50 PS)	AS 000 001	AS 109 138	AS 171 566		
Chassis Nos.	114 2000 001	114 2423 795	114 2999 000		
Chassis Nos. (VW 1303)	134 2000 001	134 2423 795	134 2999 000		

Model year 1975

Engines	1. Aug. 1974 Engine no.	31. Dec. 1974 Engine no.	31. July 1975 Engine no.		
1.2 litre 25 kW (34 PS)	D 1 284 227	D 1 309 681	D 1 347 142		
1.3 litre 32 kW (44 PS)	AR 121 272	AR 132 045	AR 150 000		
1.6 litre 37 KW (50 PS)	AS 171 567	AS 243 557	AS 269 030		
1.6 litre 37 kW (50 PS)	AJ 0 000 001	AJ 0 012 142	AJ 0 012 405		
Chassis Nos.	115 2000 001	115 2143 743	115 2600 000		
Chassis Nos.(VW 1303)	135 2000 001	135 2143 743	135 2600 000		

Model year 1976

Engines	1. Aug. 1975 Engine no.	31. Dec. 1975 Engine no.	31. July 1976 Engine no.		
1.2 litre 25 kW (34 PS)	D 1 347 143	D 1 368 488	D 1 393 631		
1.6 litre 37 kW (50 PS)	AS 269 031	AS 332 893	AS 401 299		
1.6 litre 37 kW (50 PS)	AJ 0 012 406	AJ 0 012 504	AJ 0 095 935		
Chassis Nos.	116 2000 001	116 2071 467	116 2200 000		
Chassis Nos. (Cabrio)	156 2000 001	156 2071 467	156 2200 000		

Model year 1977

Engines	1. Aug. 1976 Engine no.	31. Dec. 1976 Engine no.	31. July 1977 Engine no.		
1.2 litre 25 kW (34 PS)	D 1 393 632	D 1 410 177	D 1 415 740		
1.6 litre 37 kW (50 PS)	AS 401 300	AS 468 053	AS 526 948		
1.6 litre 37 kW (50 PS)	AJ 0 095 936	AJ 0 110 696	AJ 0 119 687		
Chassis Nos.	117 2000 001	117 2063 700	117 2200 000		
Chassis Nos. (Cabrio)	157 2000 001	157 2063 700	157 2200 000		

Model year 1978

Engines	1. Aug. 1977 Engine no.	31. Dec. 1977 Engine no.	1. Jan. 1978 Engine no.		
1.2 litre 25 kW (34 PS)	D 1 415 741	D 1 430 280	D 1 430 281		
1.6 litre 37 kW (50 PS)	AS 526 949	AS 563 435	AS 563 435		
1.6 litre 37 kW (50 PS)	AJ 0 119 688	AJ 0 126 171	——		
Chassis Nos.	118 2000 001	118 2050 000	118 2100 001		
Chassis Nos. (Cabrio)	158 2000 001	158 2028 542	158 2100 000		

Model year 1979

Engines	1. Aug. 1978 Engine no.	31. Dec. 1978 Engine no.	31. July 1979 Engine no.		
1.2 litre 25 kW (34 PS)	D 1 431 113	D 1 431 682	D 1 432 179		
1.6 litre 37 kW (50 PS)	AS 610 030	AS 644 291	AS 691 913		
1.6 litre 37 kW (50 PS)	AJ 132 851	AJ 136 982	AJ 143 096		
Chassis Nos.	119 2100 001	119 2108 687	119 2150 000		
Chassis Nos. (Cabrio)	159 2000 001	159 2018 069	159 2036 062		

Model year 1980

Engines	1. Aug. 1979 Engine no.	31. Dec. 1979 Engine no.	31. Jan. 1980 Engine no.	31. July 1980 Engine no.	
1.2 litre 25 kW (34 PS)	D 1 432 180	D 1 432 646	——	D 1 432 811	
1.6 litre 37 kW (50 PS) (Cabrio)	AS 0 691 914	AS 0 693 274	——		
1.6 litre 37 kW (50 PS) (Cabrio)	AJ 0 143 097	AJ 0 149 558	AJ 0 149 567	——	
Chassis Nos.	11 A 000 001	11 A 008 929	——	11 A 0020 000	
Chassis Nos. (Cabrio)	159 2036 063	159 2043 634			

Model year 1981

Engines	1. Aug. 1980 Engine no.	31. July 1981 Engine no.			
1.2 litre 25 kW (34 PS)	D 1 432 812	D 1 479 924			
Chassis Nos.	11 B 000 001	11 B 013 340			

Model year 1982

Engines	1. Aug. 1981 Engine no.	31. July 1982 Engine no.			
1.2 litre 25 kW (34 PS)	D 1 479 925	D 1 489 760			
Chassis Nos.	11 C 000 001	11 C 009 836			

Model year 1983

Engines	1. Aug. 1982 Engine no.	31. July 1983 Engine no.			
1.2 litre 25 kW (34 PS)	D 1 489 761	D 1 507 083			
Chassis Nos.	11 D 000 001	11 D 017 323			

Model year 1984

Engines	1. Aug. 1983 Engine no.	31. July 1984 Engine no.	1. Aug. 1984 Engine no.	31. July 1985 Engine no.	
1.2 litre 25 kW (34 PS)	D 1 507 084	D 1 523 896	D 1 523 897	——	
Chassis Nos.	11 E 000 001	11 E 020 000	11 F 000 001	11 F 020 000	

Technical data of all Beetle models

In the tables the most important technical data for the basic Beetle models are brought together. As the Beetles were steadily improved, so the technical details were continually changing. The reference date given in the tables also indicates the year for which the data became valid.

Engine performance/Compression/Capacity

Model	Engine	Year	Bore mm	Stroke mm	Effective capacity cm³	Compression	Performance in kW at rpm	Performance in PS (DIN) at rpm	
VW 1100	1,1 l / 25 PS	1952	75	64	1131	5,8	18/3300	25/3300	
VW 1200	1,2 l / 30 PS	1954	77	64	1192	6,1	22/3400	30/3400	
VW 1200	1,2 l / 34 PS	1977	77	64	1192	7,3	25/3800	34/3800	
VW 1200	1,6 l / 50 PS	1977	85,5	69	1584	7,5	37/4000	50/4000	
VW 1300	1,3 l / 40 PS	1970	77	69	1285	7,3	29/4000	40/4000	
VW 1300	1,3 l / 44 PS	1973	77	69	1285	7,5	32/4100	44/4100	
VW 1500	1,5 l / 44 PS	1970	83	69	1493	7,5	32/4000	44/4000	
VW 1302	1,3 l / 44 PS	1971	77	69	1285	7,5	32/4100	44/4100	
VW 1302 S	1,6 l / 50 PS	1971	77	69	1584	7,5	37/4000	50/4000	
VW 1303	1,3 l / 44 PS	1973	77	69	1285	7,5	32/4100	44/4100	
VW 1303 S	1,6 l / 50 PS	1973	85,5	69	1584	7,5	37/4000	50/4000	
VW 1303 Cabrio	1,6 l / 50 PS	1977	85,5	69	1584	7,5	37/4000	50/4000	

Torque/Range of torque/Output per litre

Model	Engine	Year	Max torque in Nm at rpm	Most favourable torque range from -- to (rpm)	Output kW/ litre	Output in PS (DIN)/litre		
VW 1100	1,1 l / 25 PS	1952	69/2000	1300–3000	16,25	22,1		
VW 1200	1,2 l / 30 PS	1954	75/2000	1300–3000	18,4	25,2		
VW 1200	1,2 l / 34 PS	1977	76/1700	1400–3200	21,0	28,5		
VW 1200	1,6 l / 50 PS	1977	108/2800	1300–3500	23,3	31,5		
VW 1300	1,3 l / 40 PS	1970	89/2000	1600–2800	22,8	31,1		
VW 1300	1,3 l / 44 PS	1973	88/3000	1600–3900	24,9	34,2		
VW 1500	1,5 l / 44 PS	1970	102/2000	1600–3000	21,4	29,4		
VW 1302	1,3 l / 44 PS	1971	88/3000	1600–3900	24,9	34,2		
VW 1302 S	1,6 l / 50 PS	1971	108/2800	1300–3500	23,3	31,5		
VW 1303	1,3 l / 44 PS	1973	88/3000	1600–3900	24,9	34,2		
VW 1303 S	1,6 l / 50 PS	1973	108/2800	1300–3500	23,3	31,3		
VW 1303 Cabrio	1,6 l / 50 PS	1977	108/2800	1300–3500	23,3	31,5		

Hill-climbing ability as percentage

Model	Engine	Year	Climbing ability at half load on good surface Gear						
			1st	2nd	3rd	4th			
VW 1100	1,1 l / 25 PS	1952	32,0	16,0	9,0	5,0			
VW 1200	1,2 l / 30 PS	1954	33,0	18,0	9,5	5,0			
VW 1200	1,2 l / 34 PS	1977	38,5	20,0	11,0	7,0			
VW 1200	1,6 l / 50 PS	1977	40,0	21,0	11,0	7,0			
VW 1300	1,3 l / 40 PS	1970	44,0	23,0	12,5	8,0			
VW 1300	1,3 l / 44 PS	1973	41,0	21,0	11,0	7,0			
VW 1500	1,5 l / 44 PS	1970	46,0	24,0	13,0	8,0			

Hill-climbing ability as percentage

Model	Engine	Year	Climbing ability at half load on good surface Gear						
			1st	2nd	3rd	4th			
VW 1302	1,3 l / 44 PS	1971	40	20	11	6,5			
VW 1302 S	1,6 l / 50 PS	1971	47	24	13	8,0			
VW 1303	1,3 l / 44 PS	1973	38,5	19,5	11,0	6,5			
VW 1303 S	1,6 l / 50 PS	1973	42,0	22,0	12,0	8,0			
VW 1303 Cabrio	1,6 l / 50 PS	1977	40,0	21,0	11,0	7,0			

Octane requirement/Piston speed/Engine weight

Model	Engine	Year	Octane requirement (RON)	Av. piston speed at rpm corresponding to max. power output m/s	Piston speed at max. road speed m/s with manual gearbox	Piston speed at max. road speed m/s with automatic transmission	Engine weight in kg with clutch, oil, exhaust manifold, but without generator or air filter		
VW 1100	1,1 l / 25 PS	1952	74	6,4	8,96	–	90		
VW 1200	1,2 l / 30 PS	1954	84	7,3	–	–	90		
VW 1200	1,2 l / 34 PS	1977	87	8,11	8,56	–	110		
VW 1200	1,6 l / 50 PS	1977	91	9,2	9,26	9,04	120		
VW 1300	1,3 l / 40 PS	1970	91	9,2	–	–	120		
VW 1300	1,3 l / 44 PS	1973	91	9,44	10,05	9,2	121		
VW 1500	1,5 l / 44 PS	1970	91	9,1	–	–	115		
VW 1302	1,3 l / 44 PS	1971	91	9,44	10,05	9,2	121		
VW 1302 S	1,6 l / 50 PS	1971	91	9,2	9,26	9,04	120		
VW 1303	1,3 l / 44 PS	1973	91	9,44	10,05	9,2	121		
VW 1303 S	1,6 l / 50 PS	1973	91	9,2	9,26	9,04	120		
VW 1303 Cabrio	1,6 l / 50 PS	1977	91	9,2	9,26	9,04	120		

Fuel consumption

Model	Engine	Year	Fuel consumption (DIN) litre/100 km		Fuel consumption with part load at constant speed on level with manual gearbox Litre/100 km	
			Manual	Automatic	at 80 km/h	at 100 km/h
VW 1100	1,1 l / 25 PS	1952	~7,2	–	–	–
VW 1200	1,2 l / 30 PS	1954	~7,3	–	–	–
VW 1200	1,2 l / 34 PS	1977	7,5	–	6,3	8,7
VW 1200	1,6 l / 50 PS	1977	9,2	9,6	6,8	8,6
VW 1300	1,3 l / 40 PS	1970	8,5	–	–	–
VW 1300	1,3 l / 44 PS	1973	8,8	9,2	–	–
VW 1500	1,5 l / 44 PS	1970	8,8	9,3	–	–
VW 1302	1,3 l / 44 PS	1971	8,5	9,0	–	–
VW 1302 S	1,6 l / 50 PS	1971	8,5	9,5	–	–
VW 1303	1,3 l / 44 PS	1973	8,8	9,5		
VW 1303 S	1,6 l / 50 PS	1973	9,2	9,6	6,8	8,6
VW 1303 Cabrio	1,6 l / 50 PS	1977	9,2	9,6	6,8	8,6

Acceleration

Model	Engine	Year	Acceleration with half load in seconds Manual gearbox			
			0-50 km/h	0-80 km/h	0-100 km/h	over 1 km with standing start
VW 1100	1,1 l / 25 PS	1952	11,1	28,9	–	–
VW 1200	1,2 l / 30 PS	1954	–	21,0	–	–
VW 1200	1,2 l / 34 PS	1977	7,0	18,0	37,0	44,0
VW 1200	1,6 l / 50 PS	1977	5,0	12,0	19,5	39,0
VW 1300	1,3 l / 40 PS	1970	6,0	14,0	26,0	–
VW 1300	1,3 l / 44 PS	1973	6,5	14,0	24,0	42,5

Acceleration

Model	Engine	Year	Acceleration with half load in seconds Manual gearbox						
			0-50 km/h	0-80 km/h	0-100 km/h	over 1 km with standing start			
VW 1500	1,5 l / 44 PS	1970	6,0	13,0	23,0	–			
VW 1302	1,3 l / 44 PS	1971	6,5	16,5	32,0	–			
VW 1302 S	1,6 l / 50 PS	1971	5,5	12,5	22,5	–			
VW 1303	1,3 l / 44 PS	1973	6,5	15,0	25,5	43,0			
VW 1303 S	1,6 l / 50 PS	1973	5,5	13,0	20,5	40,0			
VW 1303 Cabrio	1,6 l / 50 PS	1977	5,5	13,0	20,5	40,0			

Tank capacity/Oil change quantity

Model	Engine	Year	Fuel tank capacity		Engine, crankcase		4-speed manual gearbox		
			Total litres	Reserve litres	Oil Fill litres	Change litres	Oil Fill litres	Change litres	
VW 1100	1,1 l / 25 PS	1952	40	5	2,5	2,5	2,5	2,5	
VW 1200	1,2 l / 30 PS	1954	40	5	2,5	2,5	2,5	2,5	
VW 1200	1,2 l / 34 PS	1977	40	5	2,5	2,5	3,0	–	
VW 1200	1,6 l / 50 PS	1977	40	5	2,5	2,5	3,0	–	
VW 1300	1,3 l / 40 PS	1970	40	5	2,5	2,5	3,0	2,5	
VW 1300	1,3 l / 44 PS	1973	40	5	2,5	2,5	3,0	2,5	
VW 1500	1,5 l / 44 PS	1970	40	5	2,5	2,5	3,0	2,5	
VW 1302	1,3 l / 44 PS	1971	42	5	2,5	2,5	3,0	2,5	
VW 1302 S	1,6 l / 50 PS	1971	42	5	2,5	2,5	3,0	2,5	
VW 1303	1,3 l / 44 PS	1973	42	5	2,5	2,5	3,0	2,5	
VW 1303 S	1,6 l / 50 PS	1973	42	5	2,5	2,5	3,0	2,5	
VW 1303 Cabrio	1,6 l / 50 PS	1977	42	5	2,5	2,5	3,0	–	

Max. speed/Voltage/Generator performance

Model	Engine	Year	Max. speed km/h manual gearbox	Max. speed km/h automatic	Electrics volts	Battery capacity Ah	Generator output max. A	Generator output in Watts
VW 1100	1,1 l / 25 PS	1952	105	–	6	75	20	130
VW 1200	1,2 l / 30 PS	1954	108	–	6	70	–	160
VW 1200	1,2 l / 34 PS	1977	115	–	12	36	50	700
VW 1200	1,6 l / 50 PS	1977	130	125	12	36	50	700
VW 1300	1,3 l / 40 PS	1970	120	–	12	36	30	420
VW 1300	1,3 l / 44 PS	1973	125	120	12	36	50	700
VW 1500	1,5 l / 44 PS	1970	125	120	12	36	30	420
VW 1302	1,3 l / 44 PS	1971	125	120	12	36	50	700
VW 1302 S	1,6 l / 50 PS	1971	130	125	12	36	50	700
VW 1303	1,3 l / 44 PS	1973	125	120	12	36	50	700
VW 1303 S	1,6 l / 50 PS	1973	130	125	12	36	50	700
VW 1303 Cabrio	1,6 l / 50 PS	1977	130	125	12	36	50	700

Luggage space

Model	Engine	Year	Space in litres/sphere system 50 mm ⌀/VDA – Norm: box 200 x 100 x 50 mm					
			front		rear		total	
			Sphere	VDA	Sphere	VDA	Sphere	VDA
VW 1100	1,1 l / 25 PS	1952	–	–	–	–	–	–
VW 1200	1,2 l / 30 PS	1954	–	–	–	–	–	–
VW 1200	1,2 l / 34 PS	1977	140	127	127	106	267	233
VW 1200	1,6 l / 50 PS	1977	140	127	127	106	267	233
VW 1300	1,3 l / 40 PS	1970	140	127	127	106	267	233
VW 1300	1,3 l / 44 PS	1973	140	127	140	106	280	233
VW 1500	1,5 l / 44 PS	1970	140	127	140	106	280	233

Luggage space

Model	Engine	Year	Space in litres/sphere system 50 mm ⌀/VDA – Norm: box 200 x 100 x 50 mm					
			front		rear		total	
			Sphere	VDA	Sphere	VDA	Sphere	VDA
VW 1302	1,3 l / 44 PS	1971	255	210	140	106	395	316
VW 1302 S	1,6 l / 50 PS	1971	255	210	140	106	395	316
VW 1303	1,3 l / 44 PS	1973	255	210	140	106	395	316
VW 1303 S	1,6 l / 50 PS	1973	255	210	140	106	395	316
VW 1303 Cabrio	1,6 l / 50 PS	1977	255	210	121	100	367	310

Transmission

Model	Engine	Year	Manual					Automatic		
			1st	2nd	3rd	4th	reverse	1	2	3
VW 1100	1,1 l / 25 PS	1952	3,6	1,88	1,22	0,79	4,63	–	–	–
VW 1200	1,2 l / 30 PS	1954	3,6	1,88	1,23	0,82	4,63	–	–	–
VW 1200	1,2 l / 34 PS	1977	3,78	2,06	1,26	0,93	3,78	–	–	–
VW 1200	1,6 l / 50 PS	1977	3,78	2,06	1,26	0,93	3,78	2,25	1,26	0,88
VW 1300	1,3 l / 40 PS	1970	3,78	2,06	1,26	0,93	3,81	–	–	–
VW 1300	1,3 l / 44 PS	1973	3,78	2,06	1,26	0,93	3,78	2,25	1,26	0,88
VW 1500	1,5 l / 44 PS	1970	3,8	2,06	1,26	0,93	3,8	2,25	1,26	0,88
VW 1302	1,3 l / 44 PS	1971	3,8	2,06	1,26	0,93	3,8	2,25	1,26	0,88
VW 1302 S	1,6 l / 50 PS	1971	3,8	2,06	1,26	0,93	3,8	2,25	1,26	0,88
VW 1303	1,3 l / 44 PS	1974	3,78	2,06	1,26	0,93	3,78	2,25	1,26	0,88
VW 1303 S	1,6 l / 50 PS	1974	3,78	2,06	1,26	0,93	3,78	2,25	1,26	0,88
VW 1303 Cabrio	1,6 l / 50 PS	1977	3,78	2,06	1,26	0,93	3,78	2,25	1,26	0,88

Roof load/Turning circle/Road space occupied

Model	Engine	Year	Permitted roof load in kg	Turning circle in m	Road space occup. in m²				
VW 1100	1,1 l / 25 PS	1952	50	11	6,3				
VW 1200	1,2 l / 30 PS	1954	50	11	6,3				
VW 1200	1,2 l / 34 PS	1977	50	11	6,3				
VW 1200	1,6 l / 50 PS	1977	50	11	6,3				
VW 1300	1,3 l / 40 PS	1970	50	11	6,3				
VW 1300	1,3 l / 44 PS	1973	50	11	6,3				
VW 1500	1,5 l / 44 PS	1970	50	11	6,3				
VW 1302	1,3 l / 44 PS	1971	50	9,6	6,5				
VW 1302 S	1,6 l / 50 PS	1971	50	9,6	6,5				
VW 1303	1,3 l / 44 PS	1973	50	9,6	6,5				
VW 1303 S	1,6 l / 50 PS	1973	50	9,6	6,5				
VW 1303 Cabrio	1,6 l / 50 PS	1977	–	9,6	6,5				

Wheelbase/Track/External dimensions

Model	Engine	Year	Wheelbase in mm	Front track with drum brakes in mm	Front track with disc brakes in mm	Rear track in mm	Greatest external length without rubber buffers in mm	Greatest external height, empty, in mm	Greatest external width in mm
VW 1100	1,1 l / 25 PS	1952	2400	1290	–	1250	4070	1500	1540
VW 1200	1,2 l / 30 PS	1954	2400	1290	–	1250	4070	1500	1540
VW 1200	1,2 l / 34 PS	1977	2400	1308	–	1349	4060	1500	1550
VW 1200	1,6 l / 50 PS	1977	2400	–	1314	1349	4060	1500	1550
VW 1300	1,3 l / 40 PS	1970	2400	1316	1305	1350	4030	1500	1550
VW 1300	1,3 l / 44 PS	1973	2400	1308	1314	1349	4060	1500	1550

Wheelbase/Track/External dimensions

Model	Engine	Year	Wheelbase in mm	Front track with drum brakes in mm	Front track with disc brakes in mm	Rear track in mm	Greatest external length without rubber buffers in mm	Greatest external height, empty, in mm	Greatest external width in mm
VW 1500	1,5 l / 44 PS	1970	2400	1316	1305	1350	4030	1500	1550
VW 1302	1,3 l / 44 PS	1971	2420	1375	1379	1352	4080	1500	1585
VW 1302 S	1,6 l / 50 PS	1971	2420	1375	1379	1352	4080	1500	1585
VW 1303	1,3 l / 44 PS	1973	2420	1375	–	1349	4110	1500	1585
VW 1303 S	1,6 l / 50 PS	1973	2420	–	1394	1349	4110	1500	1585
VW 1303 Cabrio	1,6 l / 50 PS	1977	2420	–	1394	1349	4140*)	1500	1585

*With rubber buffers

Wheel sizes/Tyre sizes/Tyre pressures

Model	Engine	Year	Rim sizes	Wheel off-set (mm)	Tyre size	Tyre pressure			
						front, with half load, in bars	front, with full load, in bars	rear, half load in bars	rear, full load in bars
VW 1100	1,1 l / 25 PS	1952	3.00 D×16 4 J×15	31-35	5.00×16 5.60×15	1,0	1,1	1,3	1,6
VW 1200	1,2 l / 30 PS	1954	4 J×15	33,0	5.60×15	1,1	1,4	1,2	1,7
VW 1200	1,2 l / 34 PS	1977	4½ J×15	41,0	5.60×15	1,1	1,3	1,9	1,9
VW 1200	1,6 l / 50 PS	1977	4½ J×15	41,0	5.60×15	1,1	1,3	1,9	1,9
VW 1300	1,3 l / 40 PS	1970	4½ J×15	41,0	5.60×15	1,1	1,3	1,9	1,9
VW 1300	1,3 l / 44 PS	1973	4½ J×15	41,0	5.60×15	1,1	1,3	1,9	1,9
VW 1500	1,5 l / 44 PS	1970	4½ J×15	41,0	5.60×15	1,1	1,3	1,9	1,9
VW 1302	1,3 l / 44 PS	1971	4½ J×15	41,0	5.60×15	1,1	1,3	1,9	1,9
VW 1302 S	1,6 l / 50 PS	1971	4½ J×15	41,0	5.60×15	1,1	1,3	1,9	1,9
VW 1303	1,3 l / 44 PS	1973	4½ J×15	41,0	5.60×15	1,1	1,3	1,9	1,9
VW 1303 S	1,6 l / 50 PS	1973	4½ J×15*	41,0	5.60×15*	1,1	1,3	1,9	1,9
VW 1303 Cabrio	1,6 l / 50 PS	1977	4½ J×15	41,0	5.60×15	1,1	1,3	1,9	1,9

*Yellow and Black Racer: 175/70 SR 15 on 5½Jx15

Vehicle weight/Load/Axle loading

Model	Engine	Year	Vehicle weight (man. gearbox) kg			Permitted axle loading			
			Unladen	Payload	Permitted total	front	rear		
VW 1100	1,1 l / 25 PS	1952	730	380	1100	–	–		
VW 1200	1,2 l / 30 PS	1954	730	380	1100	–	–		
VW 1200	1,2 l / 34 PS	1977	760	380	1140	490	710		
VW 1200	1,6 l / 50 PS	1977	760	380	1140	490	710		
VW 1300	1,3 l / 40 PS	1970	820	380	1200	490	730		
VW 1300	1,3 l / 44 PS	1973	820	380	1200	490	730		
VW 1500	1,5 l / 44 PS	1970	870	400	1270	530	760		
VW 1302	1,3 l / 44 PS	1971	870	400	1270	530	750		
VW 1302 S	1,6 l / 50 PS	1971	870	400	1270	530	750		
VW 1303	1,3 l / 44 PS	1973	890	400	1290	540	760		
VW 1303 S	1,6 l / 50 PS	1973	890	400	1290	540	760		
VW 1303 Cabrio	1,6 l / 50 PS	1977	930	360	1290	540	760		

Introduction dates of Beetle and Karmann-Ghia models

VW Beetle
1945   Standard Saloon 1.1 litre/25 PS*
1949   Export Saloon, VW Cabriolet 1.1 litre/25 PS
1954   Export Saloon 1.2 litre/30 PS
1960   Export Saloon 1.2 litre/34 PS
1965   VW 1200A 1.2 litre/34 PS; VW 1300 1.3 litre/40 PS
1966   VW 1500 1.5 litre/44 PS. Discontinued: VW 1200 1.2 litre/34 PS
1967   VW 1200 1.2 litre/34 PS (Economy Beetle) in programme again
1970   VW 1302 1.2 litre/34 PS; VW 1302 1.3 litre/44 PS; VW1302S 1.6 litre/50 PS. Still in programme: VW 1300 1.3 litre/44 PS; VW1200 1.2 litre/34 PS. Discontinued: VW 1500 1.5 litre/44 PS
1972   VW 1303 1.3 litre/44 PS; VW 1303S 1.6 litre/50 PS; VW 1300S 1.6 litre/50 PS. In programme again: VW 1300 1.3 litre/44 PS; VW 1200 1.2 litre/34 PS. Discontinued: VW 1302 1.2 litre/34 PS; VW 1302 1.3 litre/44 PS; VW 1302S 1.6 litre/50 PS
1973   VW 1303A 1.2 litre/34 PS; VW 1200L 1.3/44 PS. Still in programme: VW 1303 1.3 litre/44 PS; VW 1303S 1.6 litre/50 PS
1974   Programme as for 1973
1975   VW 1200 1.6 litre/50 PS. Still in programme: VW 1200 1.2 litre/34 PS; VW 1303 Cabriolet 1.6 litre/50 PS. Discontinued: VW 1300 1.3 litre/44 PS; VW 1303S 1.6 litre/50 PS
1976   In programme: VW 1200 1.2 litre/34 PS; VW 1200 1.2 litre/50 PS; VW 1303 Cabriolet 1.6 litre/50 PS
1977   In programme: VW 1200/1200L 1.2 litre/34 PS; VW 1303 Cabriolet 1.6 litre/50 PS. Discontinued: VW 1200L 1.6 litre/50 PS
1978   In programme: VW1200L 1.2 litre/34 PS; VW 1303 Cabriolet 1.6 litre/50 PS
1979   In programme: VW1200L 1.2 litre//34 PS; VW 1303 Cabriolet 1.6 litre/50 PS
1980   In programme: VW1200L 1.2 litre/34 PS. Discontinued: VW 1303 Cabriolet 1.6 litre/50 PS
1980-5   In programme: VW 1200L 1.2 litre/34 PS

VW Karmann Ghia
1955   Karmann Ghia Coupé 1.2 litre/30 PS. Further development as for Beetle

(*PS = horsepower, DIN rating, as throughout)

       Export Limousine
1957   Karmann Ghia Cabriolet 1.2 litre/30 PS. Further development as for Karmann Ghia Coupé
1974   Production discontinued

Beetle production from 1945

Year	Date	Production	
1945		1 785	
1946	**14 October**	**10 000**	**Beetles**
1946		10 020	
1947		8 987	
1948		19 244	
1949		46 146	
1950	**4 March**	**100 000**	**Beetles**
1950		81 979	
1951		93 709	
1952		114 348	
1953		151 323	
1954		202 174	
1955		279 986	
1956		333 190	
1957		380 561	
1958		451 526	
1959		575 407	
1960		739 443	
1961		827 850	
1962		876 255	
1963		838 488	
1964		948 370	
1965		1 090 863	
1966		1 080 165	
1967		925 787	
1968		1 136 134	
1969		1 219 314	
1970		1 196 099	
1971		1 291 612	
1972	**17 February**	**15 007 034**	**Beetles (World Record)**
1972		1 220 686	
1973		1 206 018	
1974		791 053	
1975		441 116	
1976		383 277	
1977		258 634	
1978		271 673	
1979		263 340	
1980		236 177	
1981	**15 May**	**20 000 000**	**Beetles**
1981		157 505	
1982		138 091	
1983		119 745	
1984		118 000	
1985		86 457	
1986		46 633	
1987		17 166	

237

Beetle price changes from 1948

Because of the mulltiplicity of Beetle models, prices quoted are those of the most favourably priced version

Effective from:		Lowest price = 100
1. 6. 48	$\frac{RM}{DM}$ 5 300.–	139.8
1. 7. 49	DM 4 800.–	126.6
15. 10. 50	DM 4 400.–	116.1
1. 9. 51	DM 4 600.–	121.4
1. 1. 53	DM 4 400.–	116.1
19. 3. 53	DM 4 150.–	109.5
10. 3. 54	DM 3 950.–	104.2
6. 8. 55	DM 3 790.–	100.0
15. 9. 61	DM 3 810.–	100.5
1. 4. 62	DM 4 200.–	110.8
1. 11. 64	DM 4 290.–	113.2
1. 8. 65	DM 4 485.–	118.3
30. 3. 66	DM 4 635.–	122.3
9. 1. 67	DM 4 485.–	118.3
1. 1. 68	DM 4 484.–	118.3
1. 7. 68	DM 4 525.–	119.4
19. 1. 70	DM 4 695.–	123.9
16. 12. 70	DM 4 945.–	130.5
23. 8. 71	DM 5 045.–	133.1
17. 1. 72	DM 5 290.–	139.6
21. 8. 72	DM 5 390.–	142.2

Effective from:		Lowest Price = 100
19. 2. 73	5 590.–	147.5
13. 8. 73	DM 5 650.–	149.1
11. 3. 74	DM 6 045.–	159.5
13. 5. 74	DM 6 395.–	168.7
1. 1. 75	DM 6 620.–	174.7
7. 4. 75	DM 6 950.–	183.4
4. 8. 75	DM 6 995.–	184.6
29. 3. 76	DM 7 480.–	197.4
28. 3. 77	DM 7 785.–	205.4
1. 1. 78	DM 7 865.–	207.5
2. 5. 78	DM 8 145.–	214.9
12. 3. 79	DM 8 380.–	221.1
1. 5. 79	DM 8 430.–	222.4
1. 7. 79	DM 8 505.–	224.4
10. 3. 80	DM 9 025.–	238.1
11. 5. 81	DM 9 380.–	246.5
29. 6. 81	DM 9 435.–	248.9
14. 12. 81	DM 9 655.–	254.7
29. 2. 82	DM 9 895.–	261.0
17. 1. 83	DM 9 395.–	247.9
18. 4. 83	DM 9 675.–	255,3
3. 2. 84	DM 9 990.–	263,5
5. 11. 84	DM 10 525.–	277,7

(RM refers to old German currency, before introduction of the Deutschemark)

New Beetle registrations in West Germany

Year	VW Beetle	Beetle Cabrio	Karmann Ghia	VW 181	[1]	Total	147[2]
1948	–	–	–	–	–	8 184	–
1949	–	–	–	–	–	32 557	–
1950	–	–	–	–	–	50 562	–
1951	–	–	–	–	–	58 469	–
1952	–	–	–	–	–	71 440	–
1953	85 515	3 642	–	–	–	89 157	–
1954	109 441	3 728	–	–	–	113 169	–
1955	125 090	3 597	–	–	–	128 687	–
1956	138 806	3 173	4 373	–	–	146 352	–
1957	156 772	4 009	3 792	–	–	164 573	–
1958	181 306	4 708	5 044	–	–	191 058	–
1959	223 225	5 009	5 829	–	–	234 063	–
1960	292 986	4 702	6 543	–	–	304 231	–
1961	344 108	4 821	6 701	–	–	355 630	–
1962	363 955	2 266	12 378	–	–	378 599	–
1963	306 468	1 715	12 483	–	–	320 666	–
1964	339 257	1 820	13 121	–	–	354 198	–
1965	316 302	2 225	9 694	–	–	328 221	323
1966	270 273	2 224	10 198	–	–	282 695	555
1967	256 493	1 692	5 372	–	–	263 557	411
1968	259 276	2 174	4 282	–	–	265 732	541
1969	311 323	3 013	3 496	43	1	317 876	570
1970	323 513	5 202	3 421	1 048	–	333 184	771
1971	285 432	5 880	2 798	473	139	294 722	1 107
1972	252 436	5 306	1 728	338	75	259 883	253
1973	232 055	4 253	1 030	211	124	237 673	59
1974	118 915	2 596	50	303	183	122 047	6
1975	41 070	2 075	–	366	4	43 515	–
1976	15 914	3 207	–	351	–	19 472	–
1977	6 524	4 000	–	244	–	10 768	–
1978	10 876	5 450	–	196	–	16 522	–
1979	14 650	6 276	–	143	–	21 069	–
1980	9 364	324	–	29	–	9 717	–
1981	9 336	–	–	–	–	9 336	–
1982	6 271	–	–	–	–	6 271	–
1983	12 622	–	–	–	–	12 622	–
1984	11 061	–	–	–	–	11 061	–
1985	5 087	–	–	–	–	5 087	–
1986	13 043	–	–	–	–	13 043	–
Total	**5 448 765**	99 087	112 333	3 716	526	5 885 668	4 596

[1] = others: probably VW 1600 Beetles intended for later export to the USA, supplied and registered in West Germany

VW 181 = multipurpose vehicle based on the Type 1

147[2] = delivery vans built by the Westfalia company for the West German Post Office; based on the Karmann Ghia (as opposed to the Beetle Model 14 with widened floorpan)